Elite • 238

Battle Tactics of the American Revolution

ROBBIE MACNIVEN

ILLUSTRATED BY ADAM HOOK
Series editors Martin Windrow & Nick Reynolds

OSPREY PUBLISHING
Bloomsbury Publishing Plc
Kemp House, Chawley Park, Cumnor Hill, Oxford OX2 9PH, UK
29 Earlsfort Terrace, Dublin 2, Ireland
1385 Broadway, 5th Floor, New York, NY 10018, USA
E-mail: info@ospreypublishing.com
www.ospreypublishing.com

OSPREY is a trademark of Osprey Publishing Ltd

First published in Great Britain in 2021

© Osprey Publishing Ltd, 2021

A catalog record for this book is available from the British Library.

ISBN: PB 9781472845450; eBook 9781472845467;
ePDF 9781472845436; XML 9781472845443

21 22 23 24 25   10 9 8 7 6 5 4 3 2 1

Editor: Nick Reynolds
Index by Rob Munro
Typeset by PDQ Digital Media Solutions, Bungay, UK
Printed and bound in India by Replika Press Private Ltd.

Osprey Publishing supports the Woodland Trust, the UK's leading woodland
conservation charity.

To find out more about our authors and books visit
www.ospreypublishing.com. Here you will find extracts, author
interviews, details of forthcoming events and the option to sign up for
our newsletter.

Author's note

Throughout I have attempted to use the term "Germans" when referring to
the broad collection of troops from the Germanic states, and "Hessians"
only when discussing troops specifically from Hessen-Cassel. While
Hessians made up a little under two-thirds of the hired troops sent to the
colonies, and saw the lion's share of the fighting, not all German troops
fought identically to the Hessians. It should also be noted that the concept
of "Germany" as a single nation-state did not exist until the 19th century.

Artist's note

Readers may care to note that the original paintings from which the color
plates in this book were prepared are available for private sale. All
reproduction copyright whatsoever is retained by the publishers. All
inquiries should be addressed to:

scorpiopaintings@btinternet.com

The publishers regret that they can enter into no correspondence upon
this matter.

Front-cover illustration: *The Death of General Mercer at the Battle of
Princeton, January 3, 1777,* by John Trumbull (1756–1843). (GL Archive/
Alamy Stock Photo)

Title-page photograph: Owing to the terrain in North America, artillery
was not able to play as great a role on the battlefield as it did in Europe.
Despite this, artillery was still the most destructive arm of the American
Revolutionary War, and developing the use of field artillery in close support
of infantry elements over difficult, contested terrain was a challenge faced
by both sides. (John Greim/LightRocket via Getty Images)

CONTENTS

INTRODUCTION   4

THE BRITISH ARMY   6
Linear tactics ▪ Reality and modifications in America ▪ Musketry ▪ The bayonet ▪ Grenadiers and light infantry ▪ Cavalry ▪ Artillery ▪ Loyalists ▪ Irregular warfare and Native American allies

THE CONTINENTAL ARMY   25
Organization and reform ▪ Standardized drill and Steuben's manual ▪ Linear warfare
Defensive tactics ▪ Musketry and the rifle ▪ The bayonet ▪ Militia ▪ State troops ▪ Cavalry ▪ Artillery

GERMAN STATE ARMIES   46
Hessian organization ▪ Tactical limitations in America ▪ Other German states ▪ Cavalry
Artillery ▪ *Jäger*

THE FRENCH ARMY   54
Assault columns ▪ Cavalry ▪ Artillery

BIBLIOGRAPHY   62

INDEX   64

BATTLE TACTICS OF THE AMERICAN REVOLUTION

INTRODUCTION

This contemporary image gives a good indication of the diversity of troops under the command of Continental Army generals. Besides the infantrymen on the left (one of whom belongs to the Rhode Island Regiment, one of the few African-American units in the Continental Army), the two figures on the right depict a rifle-armed figure in a hunting shirt and an artillerist. (Anne S.K. Brown Military Collection, Brown University Library)

The American Revolutionary War (1775–83) pitted a huge array of opposed factions against one another in the largest conflict to take place in North America up to that point. Over the course of the war, combatants fought through the full gamut of 18th-century Western warfare. Armies traded body blows in pitched battles, skirmishers engaged one another in dense woodland, covert nighttime attacks resulted in massacres committed at bayonet point, amphibious operations were conducted under the thunder of naval broadsides, guerrilla ambushers struck from forests and swamps, and towns and fortresses were surrounded by the sprawling works of conventional sieges. The only factor that came close to matching the diversity of combat experiences during the war was the diversity of its combatants. On the side of the British Empire, British Army regulars served alongside

American Loyalist militia, American Provincials, Native American allies, escaped slaves, and soldiers from several German states. Against them were arrayed Patriots – the Continental Army, militia, and state forces – their own Native American allies, and the standing militaries of France and Spain.

The varied tactical doctrines and past experiences of these groups were put to test in the North American crucible. Military commanders had long understood that strictly European-style conflict was impossible in Britain's Thirteen Colonies. Too often objectives were too far flung, roads too poorly developed, forests too dense, and waterways too wide and rapid for the easy maneuver of large armies. Logistics were difficult to maintain and the frontier wilderness could prove inimical to even modest bodies of men. The past military undertakings of both British and American soldiers in the French and Indian War (1754–63) served as an example of how to make war in colonial America – at a tactical level, soldiers had to become more self-reliant, comfortable engaging in difficult terrain, confident enough to conduct sudden advances and retreats, and not rely on the constant oversight of senior officers. Initiative was key.

While much has been made of the different experiences of American and European warfare in the 18th century, in many ways the American Revolutionary War was also the most European of all conflicts fought in the American colonies. While numerically small compared to their European counterparts, standing armies did engage in pitched battles with as much frequency as they did in wars outside of North America. Though the conflict was frequently one of raids, ambushes, skirmishes, and clashes of outposts, it was also one of linear engagements between regular troops and standard siege operations that would have been familiar to any European military engineer. While combating the natural terrain proved challenging, armies still marched and fought in a style that often conformed with the tactical norms of 18th-century Western warfare.

The resultant conflict witnessed a blend of tactics born out of experience and necessity. In striving to gain an edge, armies modified how they fought and continuously strove to adapt to both their enemies and their environment. The result was a war unlike any other experienced by either Britain or America.

The success of the British campaign in and around New York from July 1776 to March 1777 emphasized the important advantage conferred by the possession of naval supremacy. As a result of the Royal Navy's activities, British land forces were able to redeploy with ease across the waterways around Manhattan Island, cutting off prepared Patriot defensive positions and frequently threatening to isolate Washington's main force. (DE AGOSTINI PICTURE LIBRARY/Getty Images)

THE BRITISH ARMY

A veteran of the Seven Years' War, General William Howe was a tactical innovator who fully understood that campaigning in North America required a different style of warfare. He greatly adapted the British army stationed there, particularly from 1776 onward, optimizing everything from tactical doctrine to uniform regulations. (De Agostini/Getty Images)

For most of the 18th century, Britain's standing land forces were organized into two "Establishments" – the British and Irish. This covered the infantry and cavalry regiments, but it did not account for the soldiers of the sovereign's personal guard, which at the time of the American Revolutionary War was composed of three infantry and two cavalry regiments. Nor did it include the marines (lacking the "Royal" appellation until 1802), who were part of the Royal Navy, nor the artillery – divided into the Royal Artillery and the Royal Regiment of Irish Artillery respectively – which technically fell under the jurisdiction of the Board of Ordnance.

The vast majority of Britain's 18th-century soldiers were able-bodied volunteers. Most were in their early to mid-twenties when they joined and were often motivated to do so by social and economic factors. They tended to be unskilled laborers or those working in low-income professions, men who saw the military as something that would keep them regularly employed. Some were driven by a sense of adventure, others by patriotism for king and country. While the requirement for commissions to be purchased ensured a degree of classism within the ranks of the British Army's officer corps, it should not be assumed that commanders were amateurs or dilettantes. Incompetence was rarely tolerated, and officers were expected to be wholly conversant in terms of drill and well-read on matters of military theory.

Britain's land forces underwent a number of changes during the 1760s. A new drill manual was introduced in 1764 and a new uniform warrant issued in 1768. Following the end of the Seven Years' War, the British Army was substantially reduced in size from its wartime footing. That process was reversed as unrest in the American colonies increased in the 1770s, with further reforms such as the re-introduction of dedicated light-infantry companies helping to prepare for the coming conflict.

Despite this, mobilization was slow. It took several years to train new recruits properly, and to cover the initial shortfall Britain was forced to call upon a number of German states for military assistance. By the height of the American Revolutionary War the British Army had grown to around 121,000 men serving in over 100 regiments operating from the Channel Islands to Gibraltar, from India to the Caribbean and Canada.

Linear tactics

As with all major European militaries during the 18th century, the British Army's primary battlefield tactics revolved around linear combat. A typical deployment involved infantry battalions arrayed in a first and second line with a reserve, supported by interspersed artillery and with cavalry regiments placed on both flanks. These lines were ideally separated by several hundred yards.

The British Army's primary combat unit tended to be the battalion, rather than the regiment. While regiments often consisted of two battalions (sometimes as many as four), it was extremely rare for these to be deployed together – they were typically either sent to different theaters of war, or one was used as a holding force that remained in Britain or Ireland. Because of this the titles "battalion" and "regiment" were largely interchangeable for most engagements, with a single battalion likewise being its regiment's sole presence in any given battle.

On paper, a British Army battalion's strength during the American Revolutionary War consisted of ten companies, each composed of a captain, two or three lieutenants, three sergeants, three corporals, two drummers, and 56 privates, giving a total strength of around 680 officers and men. In reality, however, the strength of battalions serving in America during the war was quite different from this ideal establishment – death (whether via combat or disease), desertion, the difficulties of raising and transporting new recruits, and the fact that the flank companies were often separated from their parent battalions meant that they rarely numbered more than 400 effectives on campaign, and sometimes consisted of only around 200. Regardless of their exact size, of the ten companies that constituted a battalion eight were "line" or "hat" companies of regular soldiers, while two were specialist – the light infantry and the grenadiers. Ostensibly the light infantry were shorter men prized for their athleticism, stamina, marksmanship, and independent initiative, while the grenadiers were picked for their height, build, bravery, and their usefulness as shock troops. Drawn up in line, the light infantry would form as the extreme left-hand company, the grenadiers on the extreme right, with the other eight companies arrayed between them, hence the name "flank" companies.

Howe's successor as the British commander-in-chief, General Sir Henry Clinton, admitted to concern over his predecessor's tactical doctrines on a number of occasions, believing that on a European battlefield they would lead British forces to destruction. Despite this, Clinton understood their value in North America, and did little to modify the largely successful British battlefield tactics during his tenure in command. (De Agostini/Getty Images)

During the Seven Years' War the line formation usually adopted by British Army battalions had shifted from three ranks to two. This increased the frontage presented by a battalion and gave it the ability to outflank a numerically equal enemy line of three or four ranks. Regardless of the number of ranks used, a line could be formed in close, open, or extended order – the files stood with varying degrees of separation depending on which formation was adopted. Before the American Revolutionary War, close order was almost always used when battle was joined.

British forces were also capable of utilizing a number of other tactical formations. Most commonly for purposes of movement, battalions could be formed into columns, either individually or in brigaded groups. Officers and military theoreticians during the 18th century fiercely debated the merits and drawbacks of massed attacking columns (*ordre profond*: deep order) and line formations that relied on musketry (*ordre mince*: thin order) (Wright 1983: 139). While advocating shock and offensive warfare during the American Revolutionary War, the British Army rarely utilized the column as an attacking formation, except during assaults on fortified positions. Likewise a hollow-square formation, which proved popular during the Napoleonic Wars (1803–15), was rarely if ever adopted – at the battle of Dettingen (June 27, 1743) during the War of the Austrian Succession (1740–48) and the battle of Minden (August 1, 1759) during the Seven Years' War, for example, British battalions in three ranks simply had their rear rank about-face to counter cavalry attacking from both sides of the line; a maneuver repeated during the American Revolutionary War by British infantry at the battle of Stono Ferry on June 20, 1779 (Spring 2007: 271). The rarity of cavalry – and the complete lack of dedicated heavy cavalry – operating in North America during the American Revolutionary War rendered this formation all the more redundant.

Realities and modifications in America

Thanks to the experiences of the Seven Years' War, it was already apparent to British commanders at the start of the American Revolutionary War that that fighting in North America would necessitate the use of different tactics from those employed in Europe. Early on, general officers such as William Howe recommended adopting two ranks and a looser linear formation, with the spaces between the files of soldiers widened. On August 1, 1776, Howe set two ranks and a distance of 18in between the files as the standard deployment for the whole army in North America, a formation which appears to have been the one most consistently used by British forces throughout the war. The thin, more widely spread line bore out a number of positives; most importantly, it allowed individual soldiers to maneuver easily through the typically dense, rough, or broken American terrain. It also provided the battle line with a wider frontage, which helped make up for the fact that Crown Forces were typically outnumbered in most engagements. By presenting the enemy with a looser, wider formation, a British line could better avoid being enveloped by a numerically superior enemy.

The wider battle formations employed by the British in North America also marked a departure from the European norm, it being extremely rare for a British deployment to consist of a first, second, and reserve line. Once again, manpower shortages and difficult terrain meant that Crown Forces usually went into battle with a single line and a small reserve rarely consisting of more than two battalions.

While loose formations aided maneuverability on the battlefields of North America, and the lack of a substantial reserve was born out of necessity, such a method of fighting did entail severe drawbacks. Command and control became harder to exert, and it was difficult for units to withstand sudden shocks – an accurate volley, or a sudden enemy charge – on the battlefield. The fragility of the loose British formations was best emphasized by the battle of Cowpens on January 17, 1781. An unexpected Patriot counterattack broke the main British line and, with the small reserve of Loyalist dragoons failing to charge, the overextended Crown Forces had nothing upon which to rally.

A   **THE 33rd REGIMENT OF FOOT AT CAMDEN**

The 1st Battalion of the 33rd Regiment of Foot is depicted prior to advancing at the battle of Camden on August 16, 1780. This gives a good indication of a regular British Army line battalion arrayed for battle during the American Revolutionary War. There are eight "hat" companies drawn up in two ranks – the two flank companies, namely the light infantry and the grenadiers, are absent with their respective composite battalions, as was the case for most of the American Revolutionary War.

The enlisted men of the eight companies deployed in a line of two ranks in open order, with intervals of 18in between each file pairing. Captains and lieutenants usually took up position on the sides of their company, supported by sergeants, while any second lieutenants or ensigns were positioned behind the two ranks of each company along with the drummers responsible for signaling commands.

A battalion was subdivided a number of times for the purposes of firing and maneuvering. First it was split into two wings, each consisting of four companies. Each of these two wings was then divided into two grand divisions, which were in turn split into two subdivisions, which were divided into the smallest constituent group of the battalion in the field, two platoons. Each battalion of eight companies was therefore split into two wings, four grand divisions (each of two companies), eight subdivisions (each of one company), and 16 platoons (two per company). These groupings were used depending on what mode of fire delivery the battalion commander chose, and which formation he wished to adopt.

In the center of the battalion, between its two wings of four companies, is the color party. This consists of two ensigns carrying the king's and regimental colors, supported by a group of sergeants, the battalion's first captain, and sometimes a small group of men known as the color reserve. Behind the color party is the battalion's commander, usually a mounted lieutenant colonel. At Camden the regiment's colonel was Lieutenant-General Charles, Lord Cornwallis himself, and its lieutenant colonel was James Webster, who was commanding the brigaded 33rd and 23rd regiments of Foot, meaning that direct command of the battalion devolved to its major, William Dancey. The battalion's lieutenant colonel, major, and adjutant constituted its field officers.

Inset 1: Open order became the standard formation for British soldiers in America, allowing them to maneuver with greater ease and rapidity through difficult terrain.

Inset 2: Because of the potential fragility of the open-order line and the difficulties of rapid advance in open terrain, flags were not always carried into battle. It would appear from the account of one British soldier that the 23rd Regiment of Foot did carry its colors at Camden, and presumably the 33rd Regiment of Foot did likewise.

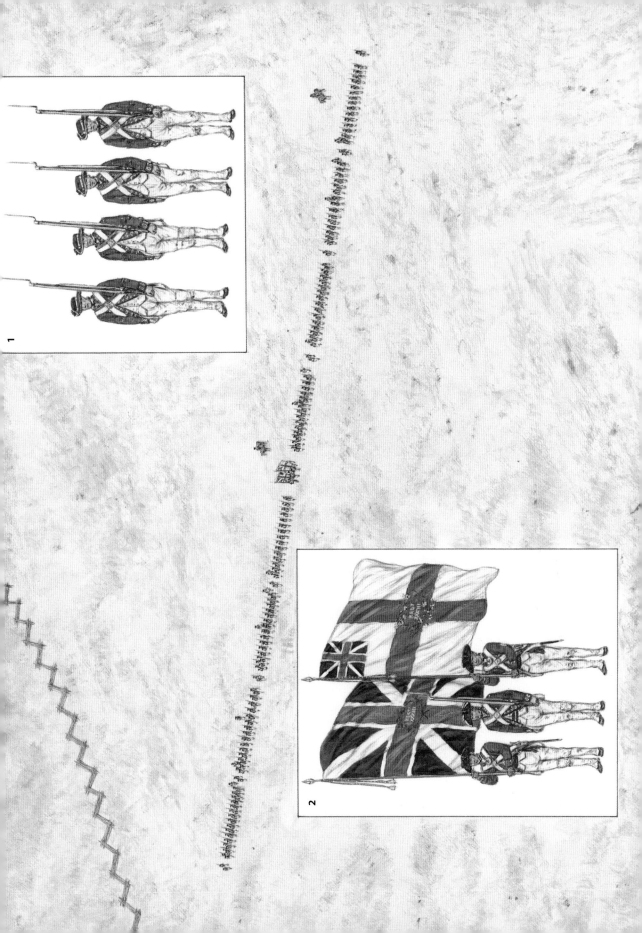

A detail from a reprint of the 1764 *Manual Exercise*, published in Boston in 1774. It shows a regiment in line and column, with the correct placement of officers. (Photo courtesy of Morphy Auctions, www.morphyauctions.com)

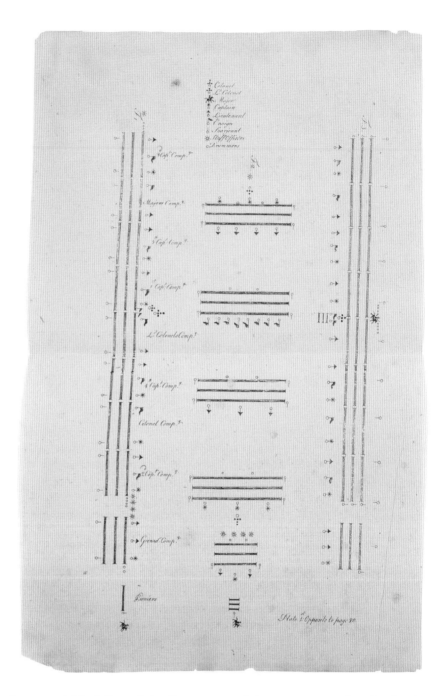

A rout quickly followed, leading to one of the most comprehensive Patriot victories of the war. Officers such as Lieutenant Frederick Mackenzie of the 71st Regiment of Foot blamed such defeats largely on the loose-formation tactics favored by many British commanders (Mackenzie 1787: 114–55).

Musketry

British soldiers during the American Revolutionary War were drilled to deliver their firepower in a variety of different ways. Volleys could be fired by battalions, either all together or by ranks. When troops were deployed in three ranks, members of the third rank would usually hold their fire as

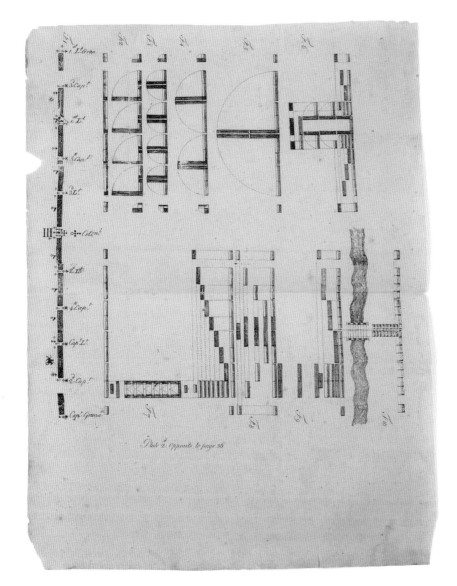

A diagram from the same reprint of the 1764 *Manual Exercise*. It shows various methods of forming from line into column and vice versa, as well as how a regiment should cross a river. (Photo courtesy of Morphy Auctions, www.morphyauctions.com)

a reserve, in case of a sudden enemy assault. Volleys could also be fired by different divisions of a battalion, typically either four grand divisions, eight subdivisions, or 16 platoons. The idea was to maintain a constant, steady rate of discharge, with no part of the line caught wholly in the process of reloading at any given time. While this was sometimes effective, even experienced troops struggled to maintain the various alternate-fire systems in the heat of combat, with firefights often degenerating into scattered shooting (Blackmore 2014: 107).

In North America, engaging a fully formed enemy in open terrain over an extended period of time was a rarity for British soldiers; and because of this, firing by divisions or even by ranks was a relatively unusual occurrence. Doing so was further hampered by terrain and the extended nature of open files. Where firefights did break out, volleys were usually delivered by companies individually and tended to occur at a range of over 100yd (Spring 2007: 202).

Debate was frequent during the 18th century regarding the merits of carefully aimed volleys versus volleys delivered at speed. Traditionally,

British forces followed the so-called Prussian school of thought that had become popular during the Seven Years' War. Such tactics placed an emphasis on firepower, particularly a fast reload rate – during exercises one Prussian battalion managed to let off six shots in a minute, a rate of fire twice the speed specified in most regulations of the time (Spring 2007: 205). While British regiments did not try to achieve such unrealistic rates of fire, there was a heavy emphasis on delivering volleys quickly in European warfare. This clashed not only with the predilection for bayonet charges that the British rapidly developed during the American Revolutionary War, but also with the views of those officers who believed carefully aimed fire was a greater asset than rapid fire.

Throughout the American Revolutionary War, British infantry were taught to aim. While there is a popular belief that Continental Army drill requiring a soldier to "take aim" implies that the British equivalent, "present," means the latter did not pick out a target, the reality is that British soldiers were urged to aim by their officers, and practiced doing so with relative frequency. The 1764 *Manual Exercise* directed that upon presenting a soldier should have "the Right Cheek to be close to the Butt, and the left Eye shut and look along the Barrel, with the Right Eye from the Breech Pin to the Muzzle" (Harvey 1776: 4). This direction describes aiming, and is little different from Friedrich Wilhelm von Steuben's drill instructions for the Continental Army (it is interesting to note that it was a committee of Continental Army officers, not Steuben himself, who specified the wording change to "take aim"). Other British officers spelled out their thoughts even more clearly, emphasizing the need for soldiers to take considered aim at their targets and thus avoid wasting their shots. British soldiers practiced by shooting at targets or marks, an activity which became regular in the months leading up to the outbreak of the war and continued for the duration of hostilities (Spring 2007: 207–08).

The bayonet

British forces in North America usually eschewed prolonged bouts of musketry in favor of the use of the bayonet. The Patriot predilection for occupying defensive positions and difficult terrain combined with the weight and effectiveness of Patriot firepower meant that British infantry quickly developed a preference for close combat over ranged engagements. The second major battle of the war, at Bunker Hill on June 17, 1775, saw British attacks faltering when troops paused to deliver ineffective fire at entrenched enemy positions; the battle was only won when a British assault finally carried the hilltop with a bayonet charge.

While British tactical doctrine in Europe tended to favor firepower, British officers quickly came to appreciate that the nature of warfare in North America necessitated speedy attacks that did not expose troops to Patriot defensive fire for any length of time. Such tactics were further aided by the initial inexperience of Patriot forces and their lack of bayonets. For the first few years of the war the bayonet earned as fearsome a reputation among the Patriots as the rifle did among the British. Typically, British tactical doctrine involved advancing briskly to contact, delivering one or two volleys, and following up immediate with a bayonet charge. Ideally, the charge itself was delivered at a brisk pace rather than a headlong rush, thus ensuring unit cohesion was not lost. For much of the war this was sufficient to panic and rout Patriot opposition.

Such tactics were found wanting in a number of situations, however. Against irregular enemies, such as skirmishing militia, the Patriots would simply scatter before the charge, reassemble once it was spent, and resume the engagement. This happened during the British withdrawal to Boston after the battles of Lexington and Concord on April 19, 1775, during the fighting around Saratoga on September 19 and October 7, 1777, at King's Mountain on October 7, 1780, and in numerous smaller engagements and skirmishes throughout the course of the war. At other times, especially as the war progressed, Patriot forces – now equipped with bayonets – learned to withstand the British charges, and even launch ones of their own. At the battle of Germantown on October 4, 1777, the surprise Patriot attacks initially drove back British troops (including an elite battalion of light infantry); while at Cowpens the Patriots routed the British from the field at bayonet point. At the battle of Stony Point on July 16, 1779, Continental Army light infantry, masterfully aping British tactics, surprised and stormed British defenses with unloaded muskets, relying only on their bayonets.

Use of the bayonet characterized British battlefield tactics but, while frequently effective as a short-term means of driving off the enemy, was found wanting against opponents with the courage either to return to the fight or to stand firm and meet the charge.

Grenadiers and light infantry

British line battalions had included a grenadier company since the 17th century. During the Seven Years' War, light-infantry companies were also added to the establishments, partly in order to facilitate the use of more irregular tactics in the North American wilderness. After the war these companies were abolished, but then re-formed from 1771 onward.

The march to and from Concord and Lexington on April 19, 1775, proved to be a stern test of British regular tactics at the beginning of the war. Shown here is the main British column, torching homesteads along the way as it tries to make it back to Boston. Scattered on its flanks are light-infantry and grenadier companies, skirmishing in loose order to keep the harrying militia at bay. Even with such tactical precautions, the column barely made it to safety. (GHI/Universal History Archive via Getty Images)

RIGHT
British Army regular battalions included elite companies – one each of light infantry and grenadiers. These companies were often detached and formed together into composite battalions. While such units proved to be among the most effective available to the British, there were complaints that removing them from their parent battalions reduced the latter's tactical flexibility and staying power. (Anne S.K. Brown Military Collection, Brown University Library)

FAR RIGHT
A contemporary sketch of a British light infantryman. Originally formed during the Seven Years' War, British Army light-infantry companies undertook skirmishing and engaged the enemy on difficult or broken terrain, such as dense woodland. Their tactical flexibility and independence gave the British an answer to the challenges posed by Patriot militia, riflemen, and irregulars. (Anne S.K. Brown Military Collection, Brown University Library)

On paper the grenadier and light-infantry companies drew from quite different recruitment pools. Grenadiers were supposed to be the tallest men in a battalion, notably brave and strong. Light infantrymen were ideally short, fit, good marksmen, and possessed an independent streak. In reality, the men of both companies performed similar tactical functions in most American Revolutionary War engagements. Drawing on his experience leading a light-infantry battalion during the Seven Years' War, Howe detached the grenadier and light-infantry companies from their parent units and formed composite battalions – three of grenadiers and three of light infantry – for the 1776 New York campaign. The exact composition of these units varied throughout the war, but most grenadier and light-infantry companies in North America served in them or similar formations at some point during the conflict.

The flank battalions were considered the elite of the army and were called upon by British commanders to fill a wide array of tactical roles. They frequently spearheaded attacks, whether in pitched battles such as at Long Island on August 27, 1776 and Brandywine on September 11, 1777, or in more small-scale operations such as the attack at Paoli on September 20–21, 1777 and the destruction of Colonel George Baylor's dragoons near Old Tappan on September 27, 1778. On the battlefield they would frequently make up the vanguard or, if the back of the army was threatened, as at the battle of Monmouth Courthouse on June 28, 1778, the rearguard. Light infantry were expected to be able to fight fully formed, like any other line battalion, though they also acted as skirmishers – they could screen the army on the march or during deployment, protect the flanks, and engage irregular Patriot forces, often in forested terrain. In August 1778 Captain Patrick Ferguson even went so far as to boast that British troops were now superior to the rebels in woodland combat (Spring 2007: 253). While as a general statement this may have been an exaggeration, overall the regulars were capable of engaging Patriot forces in broken countryside thanks to the efforts of the light infantry.

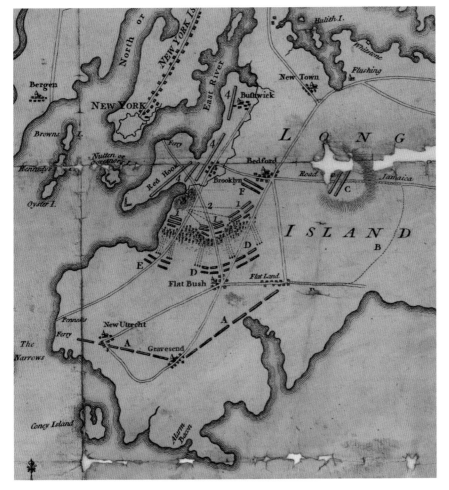

The New York campaign of 1776–77 was one of the most ambitious colonial operations undertaken by British forces in North America. Control of the waterways around New York allowed them to move more freely than the defending Patriots. A nighttime march and a flanking attack at the battle of Long Island on August 27, 1776 caught Patriot forces by surprise and almost led to disaster for Washington's Continental Army. (Library of Congress)

Cavalry

Cavalry were in short supply for both sides in North America during the American Revolutionary War, partly due to the nature of the terrain and partly due to the constant difficulty in acquiring and maintaining suitable mounts. Only two British cavalry regiments, the 16th and 17th Light Dragoons, were deployed to the Thirteen Colonies during the conflict. Because of their relative scarcity, what cavalrymen there were fulfilled a broad range of roles, from acting as videttes (mounted sentinels), scouts, and messengers to screening Crown Forces on the march and taking up the position of the vanguard, responsible for detecting the enemy and overcoming their advance corps.

During battle, cavalry were typically held in reserve, either to the rear of the line's center or on both wings. The lack of cavalrymen and the scarcity of clear terrain combined with the fluid nature that was characteristic of American Revolutionary War battles to ensure there were few instances of large cavalry charges during the conflict. Occasionally, cavalry could be successfully unleashed to finish the rout of an enemy force, such as at the battle of Camden on August 16, 1780 or Cowpens five months later, but in general they were too few in number to complete a victory effectively, and the countryside was often too broken to allow an easy run at fleeing men (Spring 2007: 271–73).

The importance of well-handled cavalry, scarce though they were, came into focus as the war shifted south in 1780. Both the British and Patriot armies that engaged one another in the Carolinas were even smaller than their northern counterparts. This, combined with the fact that the British soon found their forces spread thin defending large tracts of captured territory, meant that cavalry became more vital than ever. Both sides utilized formations known as legions – composite regiments that consisted of light cavalry, light infantry, and occasionally a few pieces of light artillery. These self-sufficient units

Cavalry were scarce for both sides during the war. While fulfilling vital non-combat roles such as messengers, videttes, scouts, and screens, massed cavalry charges and mounted engagements were relatively scarce. Standardized weapon-handling techniques and combat drilling were still in their infancy. (ivan-96/Getty Images)

were able to operate at speed across the Carolina countryside, maintaining communication between outposts, quelling cases of insurrection, and often catching enemy forces by surprise. The most successful of these formations was the British Legion, a Loyalist force commanded by a British officer, Lieutenant-Colonel Banastre Tarleton. Tarleton's Loyalist cavalry, often including a detachment of the 17th Light Dragoons, supported other British troops throughout the Southern colonies, as well as providing the primary mounted force for the main army under Major-General Charles Cornwallis. They were at their most effective when utilized to hunt down isolated Patriot forces in 1780 and 1781, successfully routing the Americans at the battle of Monck's Corner (April 14, 1780), Lenud's Ferry (May 6, 1780), Waxhaws (May 29, 1780), Fishing Creek (August 18, 1780), and Torrence's Tavern (February 2, 1781). Typically, such engagements involved a forced march followed by a near-immediate charge, which was almost always sufficient to

B BRITISH DEPLOYMENT AT WAXHAWS

On May 29, 1780, a small force of around 200 Loyalist and British dragoons and mounted infantry caught up with 420 Continental Army soldiers in the Waxhaws area of South Carolina, close to the border with North Carolina. Commanded by Colonel Abraham Buford, the Continentals ("off camera" in this view) were withdrawing following the surrender of Charleston to the British on May 12. The mounted Crown Forces troops, commanded by Lieutenant-Colonel Banastre Tarleton, had been dispatched to catch and destroy the Continental Army soldiers before they could reach safety.

Here we see Tarleton's deployments after his forced march to catch Buford. They are typical of the sort of operations conducted by Tarleton in the South – the young cavalry officer relied on the speed and aggression demonstrated by his often numerically inferior corps to catch the enemy off-guard. The battlefield consists of an open forest – no real impediment to a charge by the Crown Forces cavalry. Tarleton's light infantrymen are dismounted and have been massed on both flanks (**1**), while his Loyalist British Legion cavalry support them and also form a central body along with a small detachment of the regular, red-coated British 17th Light Dragoons (**2**). Tarleton has placed himself on the left wing, giving control of his right wing to his

infantry commander, Major Charles Cochrane, and the center to Captain Erasmus Corbett and Captain David Kinlock. The British advance has been so rapid that many of Tarleton's men have fallen behind, and stragglers (as well as the unit's 3-pounder cannon) are still arriving from the rear as Tarleton attacks (**3**).

The British will conduct a single charge across the entire line. Only on the right flank of the Crown Forces are the Continentals initially able to maintain their formation. Everywhere else Buford's line will disintegrate as the dragoons sweep through, unaffected by the infantry volley fired at a range of just 10yd – far too late. As they wheel back through the Patriot forces, the Continental Army line will collapse completely. Such simple tactics yielded results for Tarleton in numerous engagements, but were eventually found wanting when repeated on a larger scale at Cowpens against a Patriot commander (Brigadier General Daniel Morgan) who took a more nuanced tactical approach.

Inset: Both sides used mounted infantry to assist force projection during the war, especially in the South. Upon reaching combat these men would dismount and fight on foot, much as dragoons had once done. Owing to the constant difficulty in acquiring horses, infantrymen were sometimes forced to double-mount with cavalrymen.

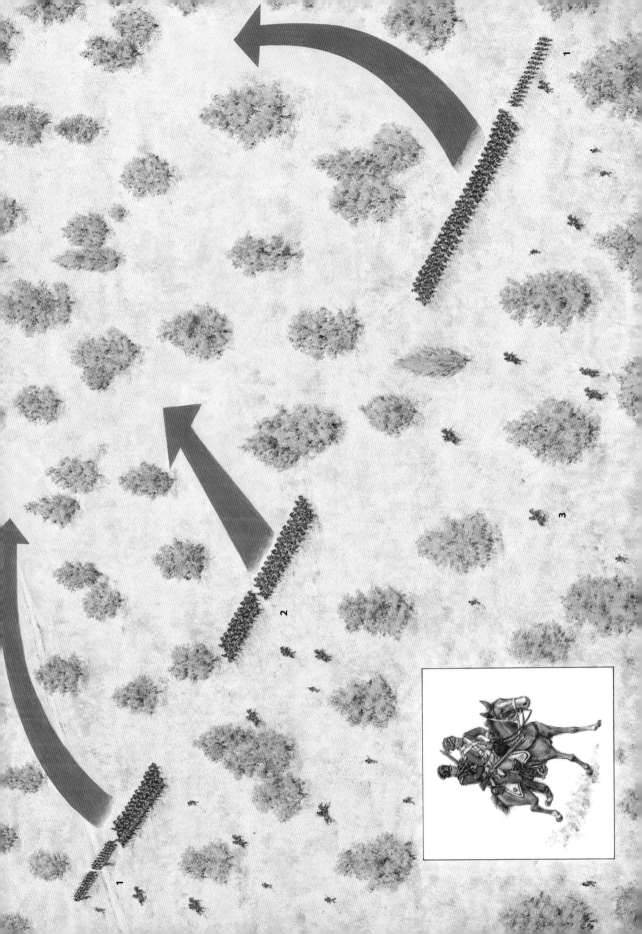

1

2

3

1

The destruction of Continental Army forces at the battle of Waxhaws on May 29, 1780 emphasized the effectiveness of even a small number of cavalry, especially when the enemy made tactical errors. Patriot infantry held their fire for too long, resulting in only minimal casualties among the oncoming Crown Forces dragoons. (Anne S.K. Brown Military Collection, Brown University Library)

rout an unprepared and inexperienced enemy. The loss of much of Tarleton's cavalry at Cowpens served to undermine British efforts in the South.

Artillery

Much like cavalry, the presence of British artillery in North America was relatively scarce when compared with warfare in Europe. The Royal Artillery consisted of a single regiment divided into four battalions, each consisting of eight companies (this number was raised to ten in 1779). During the war a single company consisted of six officers, four sergeants, four corporals, nine bombardiers, 18 gunners, two drummers, and 73 matrosses (soldiers of the artillery, ranking next below gunners) (Wright 1983: 53). Most field cannons were 3- to 9-pounders, with occasional 12-pounders, mortars, and howitzers deployed in larger engagements. At times, Crown Forces were able to put several dozen field guns to use – at Brandywine, around 20 British artillery pieces saw action, mostly a mixture of 12-pounders, 6-pounders, and howitzers (Spring 2007: 194). At Monmouth Courthouse, a total of 12 6-pounders, two 12-pounders, and two howitzers were brought to bear by the Royal Artillery's Brigadier-General James Pattinson, the most senior Royal Artillery officer in North America.

In total there were 46 cannons in the British force's artillery train, including heavy siege artillery, manned by a little over 600 gunners (Lender & Stone 2016: 320). Largest of all was the artillery force assembled by Major-General (later Lieutenant-General) John Burgoyne, whose June 1777 expedition from Quebec at first included a total of 140 cannons, 60 of which were mortars and howitzers (Spring 2007: 194). Conversely, at Camden, Cornwallis had only four guns; while at the battle of Guilford Courthouse on March 15, 1781, the British artillery consisted of two 3-pounders and two 6-pounders commanded in their entirety by Lieutenant John MacLeod.

Exactly how British artillery was organized depended on the specific army to which they were attached, but the 3- and 6-pounders were usually spread

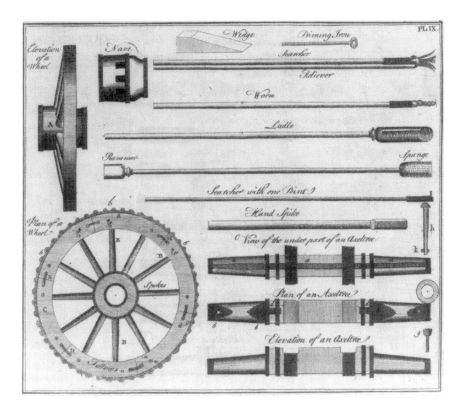

around as "battalion" guns to give close fire support to different sections of the line. Heavier guns were brigaded together on an as-needed basis to offer a base of fire (Spring 2007: 194). In most armies the accompanying Royal Artillery contingent was often divided into two separate divisions or wings.

While generally fewer artillery guns were found on North American battlefields than upon their European counterparts, artillery duels and periods of sustained bombardment were still common. The fighting at Monmouth Courthouse was interspersed by hours of cannon fire in intense heat, while almost every major action from Long Island and Brandywine to Camden and Guilford Courthouse was initiated by an artillery barrage. Artillery had a deadly effect, whether at a distance with roundshot or at close range with canister or grapeshot. The impact of cannon fire on Patriot morale, especially early in the war, was frequently telling. The desperate fighting during the retreat to Boston at the beginning of the conflict was essentially brought to a close by two British 6-pounders which, however physically ineffective they were against the scattered militia, produced a sufficiently impressive discharge to ward off the Patriot pursuit for a while. When gunners did have good targets, the results were even more noteworthy. At the battle of the Vigie Peninsula, fought on the Caribbean island of Saint Lucia on December 18, 1778, attacking French columns found themselves under fire from four British 18-pounders. The heavy siege guns had a devastating effect on the tightly packed French targets, with the Royal Artillery's Captain Francis Downman recalling in his journal "heads, legs, and arms knocked off, and bodies torn to pieces" (Downman 1898: 100). He went on to describe how "my shot in this situation swept them off by dozens at a time, and Frenchmen's heads and legs were as plenty and much cheaper than sheep's heads and trotters in Scotland" (Downman 1898: 105).

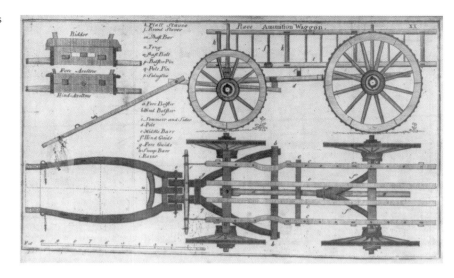

This drawing from John Muller's *A Treatise of Artillery* shows an ammunition wagon, with a view of its undercarriage and axle design. Moving artillery and sufficient ammunition in North America frequently proved challenging for both sides. Artillery tactics were hampered by logistics, and innovation was required from commanders in the field. (Library of Congress)

While British artillery was effective when properly employed, the circumstances of warfare in North America was often a hampering factor. On the battlefield broken terrain and obscured lines of sight combined with the frequently aggressive, quick-footed nature of Crown Forces to limit a static barrage to the opening phases of an engagement. Actually getting guns onto the battlefield was also often exceedingly difficult. Roads and bridges in North America were ill-suited to the weight of an artillery train – that is, assuming there were any roads at all. Guns required large teams of horses to haul them, which in turn needed to be fed, necessitating extra supplies and more intensive foraging. Ammunition was also sometimes scarce, and similarly difficult to transport. The fate of Burgoyne's initially vast artillery train is telling: of the 140 guns that started in the expedition from Quebec, only 42 crossed the Hudson River; and when battle was joined at Freeman's Farm on September 19, 1777 during the Saratoga campaign of June–October 1777, only 26 saw action (Spring 2007: 194). Generally, the complaint of Lieutenant-Colonel Archibald Campbell – that there were too few cannons compared to those of the infantry regiments on his November–December 1778 expedition to capture Savannah on December 29, 1778 – rang true throughout the war (Campbell 1984: 4).

British forces sallied out of their fastness at Rhode Island to attack Patriot forces lifting their siege on August 29, 1778. The ensuing engagement saw an effort to turn the Patriot flank repulsed, and a Patriot counterattack likewise was turned back. Ranged naval support also assisted the British. (Encyclopaedia Britannica/UIG via Getty Images)

Loyalists

Loyalist Americans supported Britain's regular armies throughout the American Revolutionary War, fighting in almost every major engagement as well as hundreds of minor ones. Broadly speaking, American Loyalist combatants could be divided into two groups – Provincials and the militia. The Provincials were modeled closely after the British Army, with most regiments even adopting red coats midway through the war in conscious imitation of the king's regiments. The standing professional soldier corps of the American colonies prior to the outbreak of the war, Provincial regiments were often commanded by British officers – a fact that some Americans resented. Their performance tended to vary from regiment to regiment. Some acted as little more than garrison units for the entirety of the conflict, while others, such as the Queen's Rangers and the British Legion, were among the most effective outfits available to British commanders.

Provincial organization and battlefield tactics mirrored those of the British Army's regulars. Militia units and Loyalist volunteers, meanwhile, acted in much the same way as the militia companies fighting for Congress (for a discussion of militia tactics, see page 37). Loyalist irregulars were most active – and most effective – throughout the South in 1780 and 1781 and along the frontier during the course of the war, where they supplemented the activities of Native American allies and other Crown Forces. At times their lack of discipline and propensity to answer only to their immediate commanders led to difficulties. A force of Loyalist Provincials and volunteers was destroyed at King's Mountain when their leader, Major Patrick Ferguson, dragged his heels returning to Cornwallis's main army, possibly because Ferguson did not wish to relinquish his independent command. Similarly, a smaller force of Loyalist militia in South Carolina was massacred by Continental Army cavalry when their leader, Colonel Joseph Pyle, delayed meeting with Tarleton and the British Legion. Tarleton and Pyle had failed to set a meetup point – a lack of planning and professionalism for which many of the militiamen paid with their lives.

Irregular warfare and Native American allies

While pitched battles in the eastern theater of the American colonies focused the minds of leaders on both sides, the reality for many combatants during the American Revolutionary War was not large linear clashes, but rather of irregular warfare – raids, skirmishes, and ambushes. These low-level engagements between small forces of men, ranging in number from a few dozen to 1,000, characterized large parts of the conflict. Such fighting occurred with regularity in the Southern colonies in 1780 and 1781 and around New York and New Jersey from 1778 onward, but it was most consistent along the western frontier, the great arc of territory that ran from Canada and the Great Lakes down to Georgia and the Floridas.

Though both sides made ample use of irregular warfare, in the west Crown Forces dominated thanks to the support of Native American nations. Britain quickly realized the value of mixed forces consisting of allied Native American warriors and Loyalist rangers and volunteers, who combined their abilities to torch pro-Congress settlements and harass Patriot forces deployed to guard them. The British were aware of the innate fear of Native Americans felt by many colonists and used this to their advantage. Native American and Loyalist commanders such as the Mohawk, Joseph Brant (aka Thayendanegea) and Lieutenant-Colonel John Butler, leader of Butler's

While the war on the frontier saw large-scale burning of homes and military structures, such activities were also used to gain tactical advantage. On July 3, 1778, for example, Patriot forces were drawn into battle at Wyoming after being convinced nearby Loyalist and Native American forces were retreating following the burning of the local Fort Wintermute. (ivan-96/Getty Images)

Rangers, used forced marches to conduct raids and ambushes, overcoming isolated enemies and slipping away before retaliation materialized.

Tactically, both the Native American warriors and the Loyalist rangers and volunteers who accompanied British forces commonly adopted a loose "half-moon" formation. Their style of fighting was fluid and irregular, relying on dense and broken terrain to allow the center of the formation to engage and feel out the enemy prior to the wings flowing and constricting around the flanks. This required initiative, stamina, and discipline to achieve. When the engagement became more general in nature, Native American forces were capable of conducting measured, fighting withdrawals when pressed close, returning to the fight once the pressure on them had been relieved – a style of fighting aped at times by Patriot militia. When a commander of Native American forces found himself gaining an advantage, an abrupt charge might rout an ill-disciplined or demoralized enemy. If the opposition were judged

C **AMBUSH AT WYOMING**

On July 3, 1778 a force of Patriot militia, accompanied by a small Continental Army detachment, marched through the Wyoming Valley in pursuit of Loyalist and Native American combatants commanded by Lieutenant-Colonel John Butler. Aware of the Patriots' approach, Butler ordered the recently surrendered Fort Wintermute to be torched in order to convince the Patriots that his force was withdrawing, thus luring them into an unrestrained pursuit.

Here, Butler has deployed his Loyalist rangers in an area of rugged scrubland (**1**), intending to fix the attention of the oncoming Patriots, who have deployed hastily from column of march to a line of battle (**2**). On the Patriots' left flank was an area of swampy ground that was assumed to be unoccupied. As the Patriot line was drawn in toward the rangers, a band of Seneca warriors moved through the marsh to outflank the enemy (**3**). The Patriots opened fire on the rangers at long range, delivering three volleys as they advanced into the trap. The Seneca warriors then sprang their ambush with war cries and a volley of their own, followed by an immediate charge against the militia forming the left flank. An order to refuse the flank was mistaken for an order to retreat, and as several officers were shot and killed the Patriot line collapsed in panic. Hundreds were killed and scalped in the ensuing rout, with only a handful of the 360 militiamen and Continentals that mounted the expedition managing to escape. The Patriots claimed the engagement was a massacre, using it to justify retaliations, which in turn led to the massacre of Patriot forces at Cherry Valley by another Crown Forces raid on November 11, 1778.

Inset: Native American warriors, Provincial rangers, and Loyalist volunteers worked closely to attack Patriot forces across the western frontier. Native American war cries struck particular fear into the Patriots and their use was a means by which to induce panic and routing.

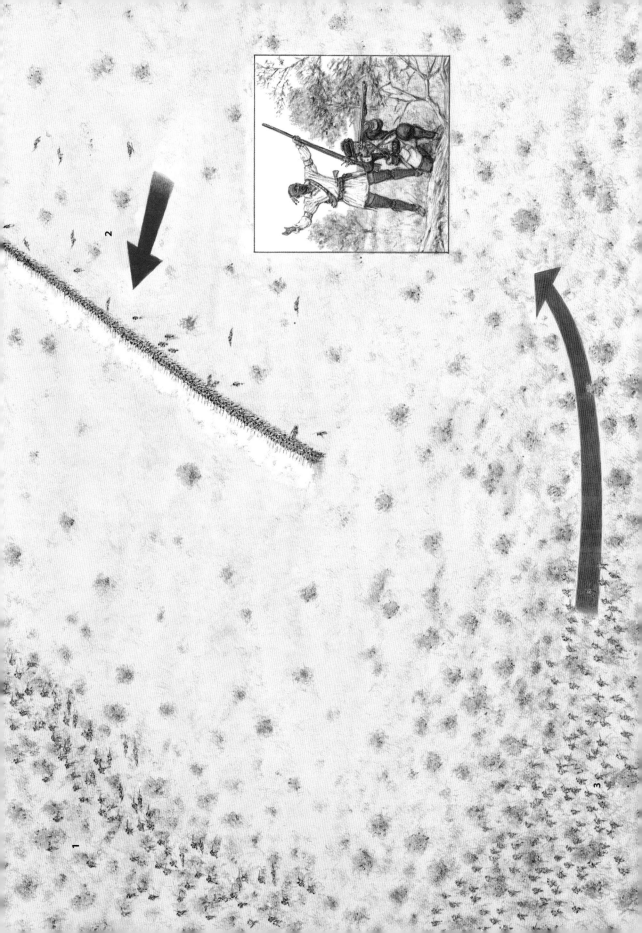

to remain in good order, a more cautious push from multiple angles of attack could be utilized (Eid 1988: 155–58).

Such a style of fighting was tactically difficult to coordinate. It took confidence in the abilities of other parts of the formation to maintain either attack or defense in broken terrain, where contact between different groups was difficult. A determined bayonet charge by the opposition could break the half-moon formation and lead to a general withdrawal by Native American forces, though such breakout efforts could also meet with disaster if cohesion was not maintained by the attackers (Eid 1988: 166). Notably, Native American contingents almost never sought to turn their half-moon method of envelopment into a full encirclement of the enemy. Doing so tended to promote more aggressive, desperate fighting – and a victory by Native American forces, even if it saw the enemy destroyed, was undesirable if it also came with a high number of casualties (Eid 1988: 158–59).

Surprise was another key to many frontier engagements. At the battle of Wyoming on July 3, 1778, Crown Forces lured Patriots into a trap by torching Fort Wintermute, which caused them to believe that the force of Loyalists and Native Americans under Lieutenant-Colonel John Butler and Seneca chiefs Sayenqueraghta and Cornplanter was withdrawing from the area. Butler's rangers were deployed to attract the attention of the oncoming Patriots, while the Native American auxiliaries laid an ambush in a marshland on their flank. Their sudden appearance led to a rout of Patriot forces, with unfounded accusations of massacre following. At Cherry Valley on November 11 that same year, the attack conducted by Crown Forces on the Continental Army garrison of the local fort was so unexpected that the fort's commanding officers, living in a house outside the palisade, were caught and killed almost before becoming aware of the attack.

For all their effectiveness, ambushes and surprise attacks were tactically difficult to implement. At the battle of Oriskany on August 6, 1777, Native American forces sprang their ambush on passing militia too soon, resulting in a ferocious running battle through surrounding woodland. Combatants on both sides utilized trees and undergrowth for cover and conducted individual, irregular fire, combined with occasional bouts of hand-to-hand combat with bayonets, knives, and tomahawks as the advantage swung one way then the other. The Crown Forces present during the battle give a good indication of the diversity of forces operating on the frontier: the engagement included warriors from the Six Nations of the Iroquois Confederation (mostly Seneca and Mohawk), Loyalist volunteers, Provincials of the King's Royal Regiment of New York, Indian Department rangers, and a company of Hessian *Jäger*, while the Patriots consisted of militia and warriors largely drawn from the Oneida, one of the few Native American nations that aligned itself with Congress at the beginning of the conflict.

British Army regulars also served on the frontier. In particular, the 8th Regiment of Foot had companies scattered in posts throughout the north-west and the Great Lakes region, providing a Crown presence to assist local Loyalists and allied Native American nations. Officers from the 8th Foot such as Captain Arent DePeyster and Lieutenant John Caldwell played an important role in helping to direct frontier campaigns throughout the war, and soldiers from the 8th Foot fought in numerous major frontier clashes, from the Battle of the Cedars on May 18–27, 1776 and Cherry Valley to the Mohawk Valley Raids of 1780–81. Soldiers of the 8th Foot participated in canoeing, walking in snowshoes, and generally sought to

familiarize themselves with the North American wilderness. They also emphasized marksmanship, to such a degree that their competence was used to put on displays that encouraged support from Native American nations. All told, the diverse forces supporting the British crown on the frontier were either threatening or in control of vast swaths of land by early 1782, a state of affairs in sharp contrast to British failures on the Eastern Seaboard.

Guerrilla-warfare tactics were utilized by both sides during the war, especially on the frontier, where mixed forces of British-allied Native Americans, Loyalist volunteers, Provincials, and small groups of British regulars proved particularly effective. (ivan-96/Getty Images)

THE CONTINENTAL ARMY

The Continental Army was formed on the orders of the Second Continental Congress on June 14, 1775. Its creation met two major requirements: the need to create a regular army from the once-disparate colonies that could engage British forces throughout North America; and the desire to provide a greater degree of legitimacy to the concept of a new, single American nation with its own – albeit limited – standing military.

From its inception, General George Washington was the Continental Army's commander-in-chief. A popular member of the colonial gentry and a veteran of the Seven Years' War, Washington led and championed the Continental Army throughout the conflict, at times in the face of fierce opposition from factions in Congress. The initial idea of a standing military was hotly debated by the revolution's governing body, with a number of

The commander-in-chief of the Continental Army, General George Washington, struggled continuously to improve the military standards of his standing army. His measured, Fabian strategies were vital when it came to outlasting the British presence and recovering from multiple setbacks. (VGC Wilson/Corbis via Getty Images)

This image from a drill manual from the 1740s, while dated by the time of the war, would still have been very recognizable to its soldiers. The new manual drawn up by Steuben included a total of 19 precise motions involved in the loading, aiming, and firing of a musket. (Library of Congress)

limitations placed on it during the early stages of the war – citizens enlisted for just a year at a time, and the Continental Army was forbidden from exceeding a strength of 17,000 men. As the war progressed and its scale became apparent, however, a number of reforms drastically altered the new military force's size and remit. At its height the Continental Army consisted of 80,000 men, with over 200,000 serving at some point over the course of the war's eight years.

Initially ill-equipped and poorly trained compared to their British Army counterparts, the Continentals adapted steadily, acquiring tactical competence and a high degree of military professionalism. By the latter half of the war, Continental Army regiments were a match for British regulars on the battlefield and were ultimately decisive in many Patriot victories.

Organization and reform

Age-old fears of the abuse of power by a permanent military meant that the Continental Army's first iteration was a modest one. Composed of three divisions divided into six brigades and 38 regiments, it recruited almost exclusively from among the New England militias, and the north-eastern colonies were its entire area of operational focus.

In 1776 the single-year enlistments first signed by the Continental Army's volunteers began to run out. This led to the near-collapse of the Army in late 1776, when the end of enlistment terms combined with a series of crushing British military victories almost to break Congress's main field force. Washington's recommendation that soldiers be allowed to re-enlist for three-year periods was approved. In 1777 further reforms expanded the size of the Army considerably, and efforts were made to standardize drill and tactical doctrine. Such changes reaped notable benefits, with Washington's forces successfully going toe-to-toe with General Sir Henry Clinton's British army at Monmouth Courthouse.

Organizationally, the Continental Army was divided into groupings classified as "state lines." There were 13 – one for each of the former American colonies – plus a 14th for Canada. From December 1776 a further 16 regiments were raised from across the states and placed under Washington's direct command. They were themselves treated as a separate line by the commander-in-chief. At a strategic level, Continental Army regiments were assigned to one of seven geographic regions known as departments. These provided a further administrative framework, but also helped to focus the Continental Army's operational planning.

In a similar way to the British Army, the Continental Army's fundamental formation was the regimental battalion. Typically, a battalion was divided into eight companies, though the number varied from as few as six to as many as ten. From 1778 onward a ninth dedicated light-infantry company was added to each battalion in a conscious emulation of the light-infantry companies already included in British Army battalions, though the Continental Army had no corresponding grenadier equivalent. At full strength a company would consist of a captain, two lieutenants, an ensign, four sergeants, four corporals, one drummer, one fifer, and 76 privates, for a total strength of

Prior to Steuben's appointment, the Continental Army suffered from a diversity of drills and commands. Steuben helped standardize tactics from platoon to brigade level, greatly enhancing the Continental Army's battlefield capabilities. (Fotosearch/Stringer/Getty Images)

90 men. This gave a post-1778 battalion strength of roughly 728 effectives, once senior officers and staff were factored in, meaning that not only did a Continental Army battalion outnumber its British Army equivalent, but the ratio of enlisted men to officers and NCOs was smaller, thereby offering enhanced tactical command and control.

As with the British, however, the actual battalion size that took to the field of battle tended to be smaller, at times considerably so – at Brandywine, for example, the nine regiments that made up the North Carolina brigade averaged fewer than 150 officers and men each, while the ten regiments under Major General Nathanael Greene, most of them Virginian, averaged about 250 officers and men per unit. While this meant they were outnumbered by the slightly larger British Army battalions, the fact that there tended to be more Continental Army regiments brigaded together offered greater tactical flexibility to commanders, allowing them potentially to outmaneuver isolated British battalions. Indeed, the use of permanent brigade formations from 1777 onward, as opposed to the ad hoc ones formed by the British as a campaign or battle dictated, gave Continental Army forces a greater degree of coherence, both in terms of organization and on the battlefield. By the final years of the war these brigade units, rather than their constituent battalions, were the core tactical component of the Continental Army in any given engagement.

The battle of Monmouth Courthouse on June 28, 1778 proved tactically difficult for both the British and Continental armies. Both sides engaged in bouts of linear warfare, with ground given and taken throughout the day as Continental Army forces attempted to disrupt the British withdrawal from Philadelphia. While this objective ultimately failed, the Continentals proved tactically equal to British regulars on the battlefield. (Buyenlarge/Getty Images)

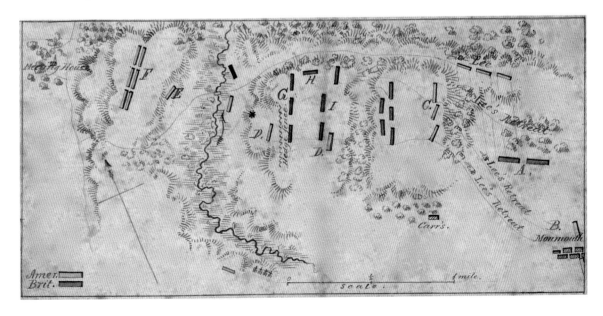

Standardized drill and Steuben's manual

When the Continental Army was first mustered in 1775 there was no centralized drill and no acknowledged force-wide practice for the implementation of tactics and maneuver. The Patriot legislatures of separate colonies – or, in some cases, the commanders of individual regiments – were at liberty to choose which preexisting drill manual to use to train and command their men in battle. Many took the understandable expedient of using the British 1764 *Manual Exercise*, but this practice was not universal. There were a number of other books and treatises popular in America at the outbreak of the American Revolutionary War, such as later editions of Humphry Bland's 1743 *A Treatise of Military Discipline*, William Windham and George Townshend's 1759 *A Plan of Discipline, Composed for the Use of the Militia of the County of Norfolk*, and Thomas Pickering's 1775 *Pickering's Plan for the Discipline of the Militia*. The divergence in specifics when it came to everything from weapons handling to battalion maneuvers hampered the Continental Army's battlefield coherence early on in the war.

Washington sought to address this problem in early 1778. He did so with the assistance of Friedrich Wilhelm von Steuben, a former officer in the armies of the German states of Prussia and Hohenzollern-Hechingen. Steuben arrived as a volunteer with the campaigning season over and the Continental Army encamped at Valley Forge near Philadelphia. Given the temporary rank of Inspector General by Washington, he embarked on a survey of all aspects of the Continental Army, followed by recommendations on how to improve everything from camp layout to the standardization of equipment. His efforts saw him given the formal rank of major general by Congress.

Steuben's greatest contribution was his attempt to standardize the Continental Army's drill. He initially formed a model company of men whom he trained personally in his own drill. These chosen men then spread the new drill to different units throughout the Continental Army – a common method of skill dissemination in the armies of the day. The drill was simplified from the 1764 manual, and incorporated elements of Steuben's knowledge of European warfare reconfigured to suit American battlefields. Following the good account the Continental Army gave of itself at the battle of Monmouth Courthouse, Steuben's drill was fully authorized by Congress, and he compiled his efforts into what became *Regulations for the Order*

This image from Steuben's drill manual shows the shift between line and open-column formations, formed alternately from the center or either flank. (Library of Congress)

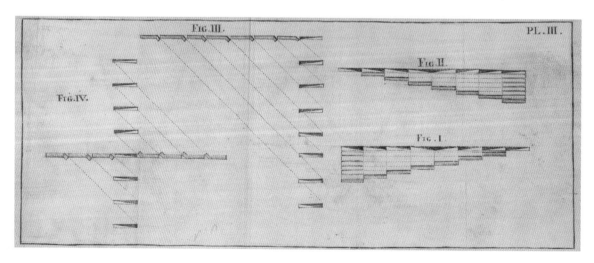

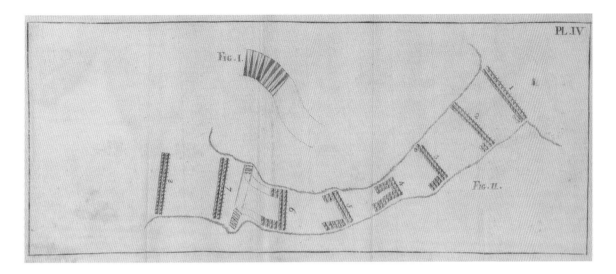

This diagram from Steuben's 1779 drill manual shows how a column should traverse a narrow terrain defile. (Library of Congress)

and Discipline of the Troops of the United States. A motion by Congress on March 29, 1779 specified "the greatest importance to prescribe some invariable rules for the Order and Discipline of the Troops, especially for the purpose of introducing an uniformity in their formation and manoeuvres ... Ordered, that the following Regulations be observed by all the troops of the United States" (quoted in Steuben 1794: 3).

Linear warfare

Ostensibly, in pitched battles the Continental Army employed tactics very similar to their counterparts in the British Army. Armies formed several lines deep, with the numerical superiority normally enjoyed by Patriot forces allowing more instances of two or three lines being employed. Battalions fought in two ranks, usually with similar spacing to British Army battalions, though there is some evidence that close order was adopted more readily by Continental Army regiments. Again, this was partly because the forces of Congress generally enjoyed the benefit of greater numbers and were not required to extend their frontage greatly to avoid envelopment, as the British were.

Interestingly, however, this could lead to problems brought on by a cumbersome advance and lack of maneuverability, factors lambasted by at least one Continental Army officer, Lieutenant Colonel John Mercer. He wrote that at the battle of Green Spring on July 6, 1781, "Gen'l Wayne's Brigade were drawn up in such close order as to render it utterly impractical to advance inline and preserve their order – the line was necessarily broke by trees as they passed the wood" (quoted in Hunt 1892: 50). The closeness of the formation adopted by the Pennsylvanian Continentals in question rendered them almost wholly ineffective, and Mercer's account goes on to describe how the British regulars opposing them engaged in their customary, looser formation: "The British advanc'd in open order at arm's length and aiming very low kept up a deadly fire. In this situation Gen'l Wayne gave repeated orders for the line to charge, but this operation was really impossible from the manner in which they were form'd and they could not push forward" (quoted in Hunt 1892: 50). Mercer blamed the Steuben drill for the debacle, claiming that "we had just begun to assume the stiff German tactics, as the British acquir'd the good sense, from experience in our

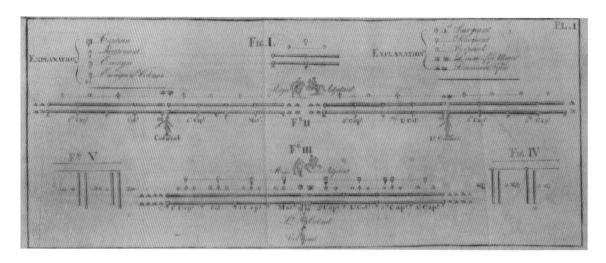

One of a number of diagrams produced in support of Steuben's new drill manual, this image shows how a Continental Army regiment would deploy in line of battle, including the positions of the officers. (Library of Congress)

This 1779 US military diagram accompanying Steuben's writings illustrates several different ways of deploying from line of battle into a column of march, including the correct points-of-view of the officers. (Library of Congress)

woody country, to lay it aside" (quoted in Hunt 1892: 50). A similar account of events at Germantown speaks of the Continental Army advance being thrown into disorder by the large number of fences and thickets (Spring 2007: 140–41).

If terrain in North America hampered the linear warfare practiced by the Continentals as much as it did the British, the effect was less emphasized due to the Patriots' preference for defensive warfare. Rapid advances and bayonet charges, while certainly undertaken by Continental Army soldiers especially as the war progressed, were less common than they were with Crown Forces. Based on their early experiences in the war, the revolution's leaders sought wherever possible to force the British to attack them, rather than go on the offensive themselves.

Defensive tactics

From the very first engagements in New England the Patriots had a strong appreciation for the advantages offered by chosen defensive positions, both natural and manmade. During the British retreat from Concord in April 1775, Patriot militiamen struck with great effect from the edge of forests, within houses, and behind walls. Belief in the benefits of defensive warfare seemed vindicated at Bunker Hill the following month

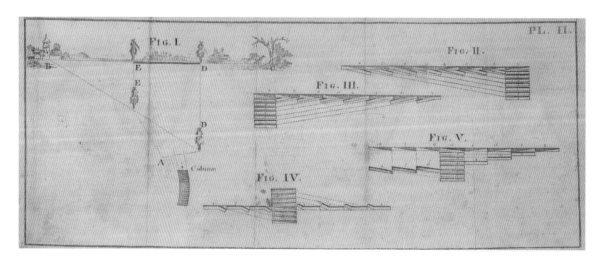

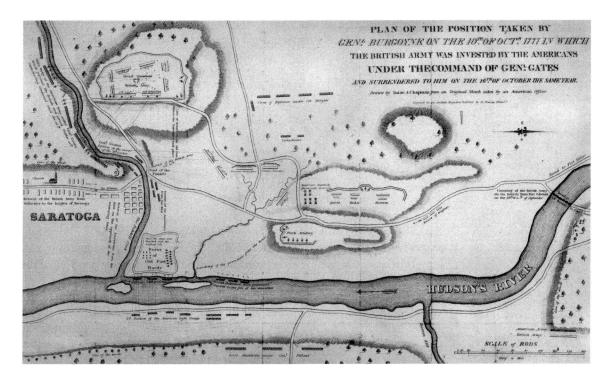

SARATOGA

HUDSON'S RIVER

SCALE of RODS

where, though the British ultimately took mastery of the field, previously untested colonial forces stood firm and delivered a fearsome death toll on their attackers.

For much of the rest of the war Patriot commanders sought to replicate Bunker Hill, though never with the same success. The British were acutely aware that they could not afford to attack prepared positions head-on. Despite the best efforts to lure Crown Forces into just such an assault, the Continental Army more often than not found itself maneuvered out of its defenses. At Long Island, Howe outflanked Washington's prepared defensive positions. At the battle of Kip's Bay on September 15, 1776, a barrage from Royal Navy ships shattered breastworks and ditches dug by the militia ahead of the successful British landing. At the battle of Harlem Heights the next day, Continental Army forces were drawn into sallying out of defensive lines, an event which also occurred several times during Saratoga. During the attack on Fort Washington on November 16, 1776, a force composed mostly of Hessians launched an aggressive, overwhelming multipronged assault that seized the fort and almost 3,000 prisoners for comparatively few casualties. At Brandywine, Washington, holding elevated terrain and a river crossing, was again outflanked and forced to retreat.

While the tactical use of fixed positions was frequently negated by enemy mobility, the defensive warfare practiced by the Continental Army was not without its successes. In particular, Patriot commanders realized that a more mobile defense in depth, rather than a force anchored to specific geographic points, could be more useful. This was apparent in the victory at Cowpens and was refined by Greene for Guilford Courthouse. Greene made full use of his numerical superiority and the surrounding terrain. He deployed three lines in depth, the first anchored on a rail fence, the second in heavy woodland, and the third in open ground beyond, partially elevated by a low hill. Though his forces were driven from the field after a prolonged engagement, such

The battle of Saratoga was perhaps the most vital Patriot victory of the war. The actions at and around Saratoga in September and October 1777 resulted from British strategic overconfidence and lack of coordination. On the battlefield, Crown Forces were unable to match the overwhelming Patriot presence and effective use of terrain, consistently failing to regain the initiative and ending up surrounded and stranded. (Encyclopaedia Britannica/UIG via Getty Images)

31

The battle of Guilford Courthouse showed the effectiveness of the Continental Army's defense in depth combined with useful terrain. Rail fencing, woodland, and a low hill were all employed to slow and break up the British attack. (Library of Congress)

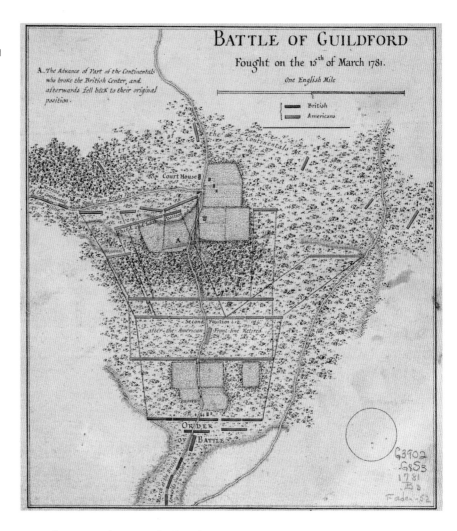

use of terrain along with the clever use of superior numbers caused high casualties among the Crown Forces. Throughout the war, the tactical defense emphasized by Patriot troops ensured that their opponents were exposed and frequently forced into aggressive, high-risk maneuvers on the battlefield.

D PATRIOT DEPLOYMENT AND MOVEMENTS AT COWPENS

On January 17, 1781, Lieutenant-Colonel Banastre Tarleton's pursuing force caught up with and engaged a Patriot army commanded by Brigadier General Daniel Morgan. Seemingly trapped against the Broad River, Morgan turned the tables on Tarleton and used his enemy's predictability to his own advantage. His initial deployment consists of three lines. On the brow of a low hill are his best infantry, Continental soldiers from Virginia, Maryland, and Delaware along with veteran militiamen and state troops, amounting to around 550 men (**1**). Before the shallow rise is a line composed solely of militiamen (**2**), with a further line ahead of them arrayed as skirmishers (**3**). Behind the low hill Morgan has grouped his cavalry, composed of Continental Army and state dragoons and mounted militia (**4**).

As was his custom, Tarleton attacked immediately, regardless of his men's exhaustion. An initial dragoon charge against the first line of skirmishing militiamen was checked. The skirmishers then withdrew before the Crown Forces infantry to join the main militia line at the foot of the hill. The Patriots fired two volleys, then conducted a tactical retreat around the left of the Patriots' third line (**5**). Drawn in by the apparent farther withdrawal of the right side of the third line, the overextended British were met with volleys and a bayonet charge. The militia from the second line had circled all the way around the hill to come up on the British left (**6**) while the Patriot cavalry, though outnumbered, struck as a single mass on the Crown Forces' right and defeated the dragoons there in detail (**7**), allowing them to assault the main British line from the rear. What followed was the rout of the Crown Forces, and perhaps the most complete tactical Patriot victory of the war.

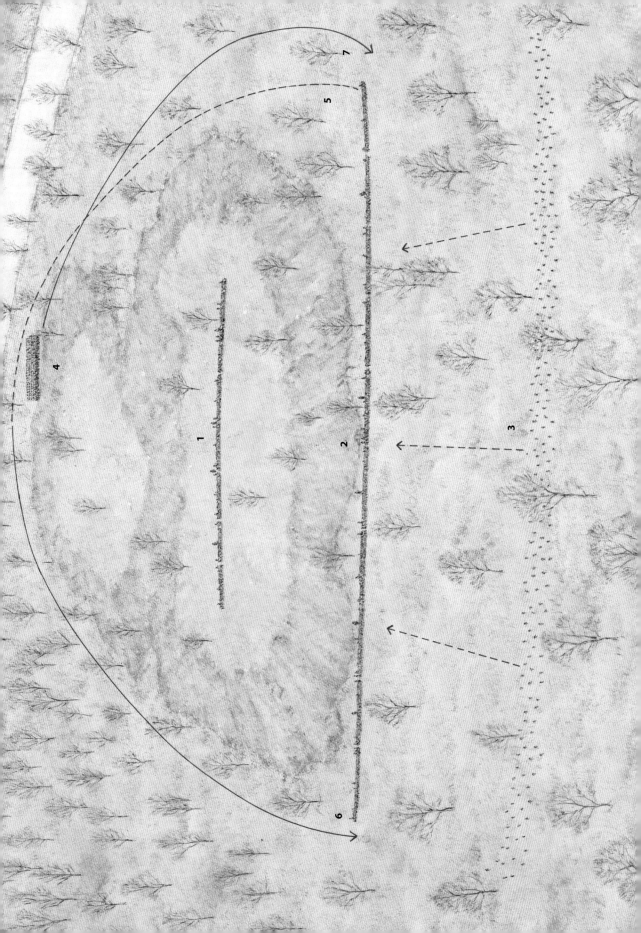

Musketry and the rifle

Traditional studies of the American Revolutionary War have often claimed that Patriot forces relied on accurate firepower to win battles. While more recent scholarship has shown that the British also placed emphasis on both weight of fire and accuracy, it remains true that fire superiority was usually the key tactical doctrine of the Continental Army during the conflict. Based partly on their predilection for defensive warfare, Continental Army forces were also able to use the numerical superiority they usually enjoyed in order to outgun British regulars.

Continental Army regiments were capable of delivering fire in the same ways as their British Army counterparts, using battalion volleys or firing by divisions or platoons. The larger number of officers and NCOs in a standard Continental Army battalion meant that regulating fire during combat – never an easy task – was simpler for the Patriots than it was for their British counterparts.

While smoothbore muskets – whether of French, Spanish, or British design – were the mainstay weapons of the Continental Army, rifle companies were raised at the beginning of the war and continued to serve throughout. Units such as the Maryland and Virginia Rifle Regiment, raised in June 1776, fulfilled the same roles of British and German light infantry, screening the main army and skirmishing with enemy forces. In 1777, Continental Army Colonel Daniel Morgan was ordered by Washington to form a Provisional Rifle Corps. This unit went on to serve with distinction during the Saratoga campaign, engaging Crown Forces from range and in difficult terrain. The irregular, dispersed style of fighting and the use of cover allowed Continental Army riflemen to remain secure during prolonged firefights where range and accuracy were the tactical priorities. While riflemen were not equipped with bayonets, they often simply withdrew when threatened by an enemy advance. Rifle-armed infantry could also target enemy officers, an act that drew some censure from the British (Hoock 2017: 75–77).

While the rifle could inflict disproportionate casualties on enemy forces and at times won battles, it was highly dependent on the right battlefield conditions being present, and a number of drawbacks hampered its effectiveness throughout the war. As mentioned, the fact that rifles were not compatible with bayonets meant riflemen were of no use in the line of battle – they required an open escape route if attacked at close range, and were not always guaranteed to come back after withdrawing. Second, rifles took longer to load than smoothbore muskets, again rendering them unsuitable for massed volleys in the linear warfare the Continental Army sought to pursue.

A particularly adept guerrilla leader, Brigadier General Daniel Morgan employed a tactical defense in depth at the battle of Cowpens on January 17, 1781 that brought about a vital victory for the Patriots. His battleplan was later copied by Major General Nathanael Greene at the battle of Guilford Courthouse on March 15, 1781. (© CORBIS/Corbis via Getty Images)

Third, rifles were generally less well suited to the rigors of campaigning, being more prone to fouling and damage. The oft-cited usefulness of Continental Army riflemen in sniping British Army officers also proved less effective as the war progressed. Shooting at officers was hardly unusual in the warfare of the period, and men had been sniping commanders at range for centuries. During the American Revolutionary War many British commanders made field modifications to their uniforms that made them less obvious targets. The effectiveness of this is borne out by the fact that one-eighth of all British officer casualties were inflicted during the fighting at Bunker Hill – but after this early engagement, the ratios of deaths and woundings in battle did not notably exceed those of other conflicts during this period (Hoock 2017: 75).

Finally, by late 1776 Crown Forces had acquired large numbers of rifles of their own. A new design, the Pattern 1776 Infantry Rifle – the British Army's first service rifle – was manufactured and 1,000 were shipped to America, to be dispersed among light-infantry and light-dragoon units. Hundreds of rifle-armed German *Jäger* also served alongside the British, and there were rifle-armed Loyalist outfits as well, from rangers and militia to the rifle company specifically raised and equipped as part of the Queen's Rangers, a Provincial regiment. Native American auxiliaries also utilized rifles all across the frontier. Ultimately, by the midpoint of the war Patriot commanders could no longer be guaranteed small-arms ranged superiority or superior marksmanship on the battlefield.

This 19th-century artwork shows a popular view of tactics used during the war – a Patriot marksman sniping a British soldier. In reality, while some targeting of officers did occur on both sides, officer casualties were not markedly higher than in other conflicts of the period. (duncan1890/Getty Images)

All of this meant the rifle was not always viewed favorably by Continental Army officers. In 1777 Washington responded via one of his staff officers to a subordinate who had spoken ill of the rifles with which some of his men were equipped, commenting that he was "satisfied with the justice of your observation about rifles, [and] has determined to have as few used as possible. He will put muskets into the hands of all those battalions that are not very well acquainted with rifles" (quoted in Muhlenberg 1849: 354). Indeed, Morgan summed up the tactical requirements of rifle-armed troops most succinctly when an officer recalled him saying: "my riflemen would have been of little service if they had not always had a line of Musquet and Bayonette men to support us; it is this that gives them confidence. They know, if the enemy charges them they have a place to retreat to and are not beat clear off" (quoted in Graham 1904: 135).

The bayonet

Initially, Patriot forces received, at best, little instruction on the use of bayonets and, at worst, were not issued with the weapon at all. This began to change around the midpoint of the war as the Continental Army became an increasingly professional fighting force. Steuben's drill manual dictated that all regular enlisted men be armed "with firelocks and bayonets" (Steuben 1794: 5). As the Patriots became more accustomed to aggressive warfare, so too their use of the bayonet became more regular. At Germantown, Brigadier General Anthony Wayne recalled how his Continentals "pushed on with their bayonets … The rage and fury of the soldiers was not to be restrained for some time at least not until great numbers of the enemy fell by our bayonets" (quoted in Stille 1893: 96). Indeed, after suffering from British use of the bayonet at Paoli, Wayne became one of the foremost proponents of the weapon in the Continental Army. His greatest success came at Stony Point, when Continental Army light infantry launched a surprise assault on the British defenses. Leaving their muskets unloaded and relying on their bayonets alone, they rapidly overwhelming the garrison and forced the surrender of over 500 men.

While such success was a standout, the Continental Army's competence with the bayonet went a long way to improving confidence, both among the rank-and-file and among officers and senior staff, who knew that a British bayonet charge would no longer automatically result in a rout. The Continental Army's ability to withstand such attacks, and launch ones of their own, negated a key tactical advantage for the British and gave the Continentals the flexibility to not only match but defeat enemy regulars in the field.

These contemporary German images show Patriot soldiers wearing the hunting shirt, a loose garment favored by Patriot skirmishers operating in difficult terrain. Not all Patriot troops were initially equipped with bayonets, but they became standard as the war progressed, giving the Continental Army far greater tactical flexibility when it came to meeting British assaults, or launching their own. (Anne S.K. Brown Military Collection, Brown University Library)

Militia

Since the earliest days of European colonial settlement, service with the local militia had been a requirement among adult American males. Local companies would drill together three or four times a year, but by early 1775 were doing so as frequently as three or four times a week. Officers were elected by their men, and throughout 1774 and 1775 most standing colonial militia companies purged their ranks of those with Loyalist sympathies. By the time fighting broke out between Lexington and Concord on April 19, 1775, militia units throughout the colonies were acting as Patriot enforcers, suppressing Loyalists and securing the authority of Congress throughout the colonies. By this time a number of senior militia leaders were also veterans of the French and Indian War. Indeed, it is possible that the average militia combatant fighting on April 19 possessed more combat experience than the average British regular who opposed him.

The initial actions of the militia on the battlefield were auspicious. Companies from New England savaged British regulars during the initial retreat from Concord to Boston, and then exacted a fearsome toll upon the king's men at Bunker Hill. In subsequent battles militia bands supported the Continental Army, sometimes in their thousands, and likewise took the lead in hundreds of smaller engagements and skirmishes. Despite this

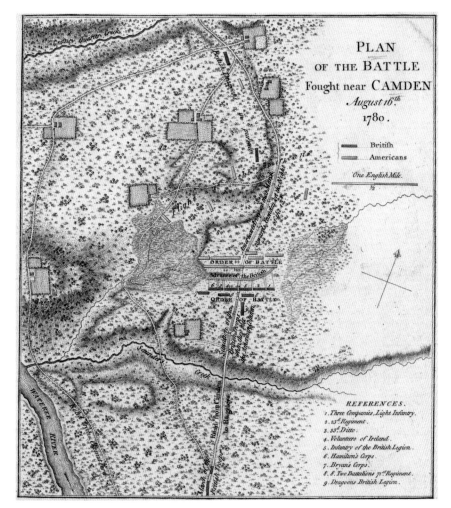

The battle of Camden on August 16, 1780 is often cited as an example of how ill-suited Patriot militia were to linear warfare. While it is true that the militia collapsed against British regulars, Major General Horatio Gates's Continentals stood their ground during a prolonged fight. Lieutenant-General Charles, Lord Cornwallis displayed a relative lack of tactical ingenuity, preferring to rely on a frontal assault. While this was successful at Camden, it would be punished at Guilford Courthouse seven months later. (Library of Congress)

This painting by William Tylee Ranney (1813–57) shows Patriot partisan Francis Marion crossing the Pee Dee River in South Carolina. Waterways across North America were of great tactical importance, providing rapid transport and impeding either fleeing or pursuing forces. A number of engagements, such as Lenud's Ferry on May 6, 1780 and Cowan's Ford on February 1, 1781, involved rivers being crossed by attackers or fugitives. (Anne S.K. Brown Military Collection, Brown University Library)

contribution, opinion as to the tactical usefulness of the militia for the Patriot cause sharply divided both members of Congress and officers in the Continental Army, not least of them Washington.

The popular image of the militia during the American Revolutionary War is of a grizzled frontiersman, clad in a hunting shirt or buckskin and armed with a Pennsylvania long rifle. While such a view did roughly represent a sizable minority, the reality is that most militiamen hailed from established towns and farms rather than the western wilderness, and probably a little over half were armed with smoothbore muskets or fowling pieces. Militia companies included men of all ages from numerous different trades and backgrounds which, when combined with their geographic diversity when different units gathered together under a single command, goes some way to explaining the mixed results achieved by militia on the battlefield.

At times, militia were the decisive element in any given engagement. At Saratoga thousands of militiamen flocked to reinforce Lieutenant General Horatio Gates's Continental Army forces. Engaging the British in forested terrain, skirmishing, and withdrawing when threatened, they helped maneuver Crown Forces into the first major defeat for a British field army

E PATRIOT MILITIA ATTACK AT KING'S MOUNTAIN

On October 7, 1780, a Loyalist force commanded by the British Major Patrick Ferguson was surrounded and overrun at King's Mountain, South Carolina. Their attackers consisted of around 900 militiamen from the western regions of the Carolinas, including a group of so-called "Overmountain Men" from the frontier settlements west of the Appalachian Mountains. The Patriot militia companies had rallied to oppose the progress of Ferguson's Loyalists, and had caught up with him after a forced march that had carried them through the night.

The militia are divided into seven companies that almost encircled King's Mountain, a forested, rocky hill shaped similarly to a footprint, with the highest rise, King's Pinnacle, at its the heel. The Loyalists have encamped at the lower, rounded side (1). The ensuing battle would display the bushfighting tactics and loose command-and-control style that brought the best out of militia forces during the American Revolutionary War. Each of the seven Patriot companies operates independently throughout the battle, using trees, rocks, and undergrowth to skirmish with the Loyalists near the top of the hill. Where resistance is weak the Patriots press close (2). Ferguson has responded by ordering a number of bayonet charges downhill (3). While these will cause the Patriots to

withdraw, once the Loyalist charge is spent and they withdraw back toward the crest, the Patriots will simply return and resume the battle. All the while other companies continue to press the attack, maintaining a relentless pressure around the hill. Ferguson would be killed as he tried to break out and his command collapsed, resulting in the death or capture of almost the entire Loyalist force.

The use of irregular warfare in forested terrain provided militia with cover and concealment and gave them opportunities to withdraw when threatened with superior force. Similar tactics to those used at King's Mountain were employed throughout the war at engagements such as Freeman's Farm. When they were required to fight in line in open terrain, militia were best used as part of a defense in depth, as at Cowpens and Guilford Courthouse. When going toe-to-toe with regulars in a linear engagement, such as at Camden, militia were almost guaranteed to come off worse.

Inset: Not all of the Patriot militiamen at King's Mountain were frontiersmen in hunting shirts and from beyond the Appalachian Mountains. Throughout the war, militiamen on both sides could be found from every trade and level of social strata in the colonies. Their effectiveness depended very much on how they were employed tactically by their commanders.

during the war. Frontiersmen used similar tactics to destroy a large Loyalist detachment at King's Mountain. There were also, though, cases where the militia withdrew and refused to return to the fight, or just generally avoided becoming engaged in developing clashes. For example, there were militia nearby at both Paoli and the massacre of Baylor's dragoons at Old Tappan, but in both cases they failed to give any assistance to Continental Army forces when they were attacked. At the battle of White Plains on October 28, 1776, militia twice retreated from defensive positions and exposed Continental Army regulars to being outflanked, while at the battle of Bound Brook on April 13, 1777, militia largely abandoned the badly outnumbered Pennsylvanian Continental Army infantry and artillery. Their natural lack of professional military experience also resulted in defeats that might otherwise have been avoided. Militia stationed near Hancock's Bridge in New Jersey were massacred on March 21, 1778 by Loyalist Provincials after they failed to set sufficient guards. Such unreliability both on the battlefield and off it led to Washington writing on September 30, 1776: "I am wearied to death all day with a variety of perplexing circumstances, disturbed at the conduct of the militia, whose behavior and want of discipline has done great injury to the other troops, who never had officers, except in a few instances, worth the bread they eat" (Quoted in Dean, Green, & Smith 1873: 54).

Fighting in the Carolinas in 1780 and 1781 emphasized the best and the worst of the militia's contribution to the Patriot cause. After the fall of Charleston on May 12, 1780 and the destruction of Colonel Abraham Buford's Continental Army forces 17 days later, there was no centrally organized resistance to the resurgent Crown Forces in the Southern colonies. Despite this, Patriot militia continued to band together to resist the efforts of Cornwallis as he sought to extend British control over first South Carolina and then North Carolina. Patriot commanders such as Lieutenant Colonel Elijah Clark, Brigadier General Thomas Sumter, Colonel Isaac Shelby, Lieutenant Colonel Francis Marion, Brigadier General Andrew Pickens, and Brigadier General Daniel Morgan stirred up resistance against the British, putting down Loyalist support and isolating and attacking scattered Crown Forces garrisons. Conversely, this resistance precipitated a slide into anarchy, with summary executions and revenge killings by both sides fueling lawlessness and creating an environment in which neither the British nor Congress were able to exert genuine authority. Greene wrote despairingly of how "the Whigs seem determined to extirpate the Tories, and the Tories the Whigs. Some thousands have fallen in this way in this quarters, and the evil rages with more violence than ever. If a stop cannot be put to these massacres, the country will be depopulated in a few months more, as neither Whig nor Tory can live" (Greene 1867: 226).

Even worse, at least as far as Continental Army commanders were concerned, was the militia's continued tactical underperformance in pitched battles. At Camden the militia formed the left wing of Gates's Southern Army, but they were routed almost as soon as they were attacked by British regulars. The Continental Army regiments were abandoned to fight on until enveloped and overwhelmed. At both Cowpens and Guilford Courthouse, Continental Army commanders consciously incorporated the militia's unreliability into their tactics, telling them to fire off just two shots before withdrawing before the oncoming Crown Forces regulars. While the fighting at Guilford Courthouse took a fearsome toll on Cornwallis's army, 1,000 of Greene's militiamen deserted him in the aftermath of the engagement.

Though the political and strategic role of Patriot militia throughout the war was vital, their tactical contribution was markedly mixed. Militia companies tended to excel when composed of more experienced men, with able commanders willing to allow them to utilize irregular styles of fighting. When militia were inexperienced or asked to engage in linear warfare facing Crown Forces regulars, however, they tended to be found wanting.

State troops

Besides supplying soldiers for the Continental Army, individual American states maintained their own standing forces for the purposes of defense. These ran the full gamut of infantry, cavalry, and artillery regiments, mixed legions, and even navies. Such forces were often criticized for taking desperately needed men and resources away from the Continental Army. With a few notable exceptions, such as the small units involved at Cowpens, state forces were the least involved of the various Patriot armed contingents. In drill and in tactics, they deferred initially to the British methods widely practiced by Patriot forces at the start of the war, and later to the practices of the Continental Army.

Cavalry

When the Continental Army was first assembled in 1775 it had no formal cavalry regiments. Mounted soldiers were thought to be of little use in the terrain of New England, and Congress, forever short on funds, did not approve of the cost required to recruit, train, equip, and mount cavalry regiments. The role of cavalry in the Continental Army was filled by mounted militia or volunteer groups such as the Philadelphia City Troop of Light Horse, who distinguished themselves on several occasions as Washington's personal guard. Congress's aversion to regular cavalry finally changed on December 12, 1776, when a regiment of militia were formally converted into light dragoons. The following year Washington received permission to form the Corps of Continental Light Dragoons. On paper this was to consist of four regiments, each with 280 men divided into six troops. As was so often the case during the war, however, especially when it came to cavalry, such figures were never actually realized – for most of the conflict none of the four regiments included more than 200 effectives.

The four regiments of Continental Dragoons were initially commanded by Casimir Pulaski, a Polish adventurer who had been given the rank of brigadier general on September 15, 1777. With the assistance of Hungarian nobleman Michael Kovats de Fabriczy, Pulaski set about training the Continental Army's cavalry to act as more than mere scouts and videttes,

A rather unusual 1775 depiction of Patriot cavalrymen. The Continental Army's cavalry force was almost nonexistent early in the war, but those units that did exist provided valuable service. A lack of good mounts and the expense in equipping them meant cavalry remained relatively scarce on the battlefield. (Anne S.K. Brown Military Collection, Brown University Library)

The battle of Princeton on January 3, 1777 was the culmination of a vital week for the Continental Army. In a small-scale campaign, Washington used speed and surprise to strike at a number of Crown Forces posts, where his troops proved capable of both effective offense and defense in the face of British regulars. The battle also saw Patriot infantry, artillery, and cavalry operating effectively together. (DEA PICTURE LIBRARY/Getty Images)

introducing shock cavalry concepts and proper saber drills (Wright 1983: 133). As part of this a mixed force of dragoons, lancers, and light infantry known as Pulaski's Legion was formed on March 28, 1778. The concept of augmenting the small numbers of cavalry available with the addition of light infantry proved popular, and two further legion formations – Lee's Legion and Armand's Legion – were created.

The record of the Continental Army's cavalry throughout the war was a mixed one. Permanently hampered by a lack of funding and the eternal struggle to acquire and maintain sufficient horses, they acted on the fringe of the main force, their numbers often dispersed among reconnaissance roles. The tactical application of the Philadelphia City Troop of Light Horse is instructive of the uses of Patriot mounted troops between 1776 and 1778 – at the battle of Trenton on December 26, 1776 they provided protection for Washington and acted as the rearguard during the Continental Army's withdrawal over the Delaware River, while at the battle of Princeton on January 3, 1777 they mounted a charge that preserved the Continental Army's artillery during another tactical withdrawal.

While successful in the roles assigned to them, the numbers of cavalry were too few to bestow serious tactical advantages. That changed to some degree during the southern campaigns of 1780 and 1781. The smaller armies involved and the geographic separation between outposts and centers of control made cavalry a highly useful commodity for commanders on both sides. Just as Tarleton's British and Loyalist cavalry dealt a number of blows to Patriot militia in the Carolinas, so Continental Army cavalry and, more regularly, mounted militia hampered British efforts to re-establish Crown authority. Mobile, independently operating groups of mounted partisans such as those commanded by Marion used their speed to launch raids and surprise assaults, activities ably supplemented by Lee's Legion. Commanded by Lieutenant Colonel Henry Lee, the Legion – later known as Light Horse Harry – won a string of victories in the irregular war in the South and shielded Greene's army during its crucial withdrawal into North Carolina in 1781.

One of Lee's most notable victories was near the Haw River on February 24, 1781, when he surprised a force of Loyalist militia under Robert

Pyle. The green uniforms of Lee's Legion were nearly identical to those of Tarleton's British Legion. Pyle was expecting to rendezvous with Tarleton, a fact Lee discovered. When Lee's dragoons approached, they did so claiming to be Tarleton's men; the Loyalist militia lined up to receive them with cheers, only for Lee's cavalry abruptly to attack them. Pyle's command was shattered in the ensuing massacre. Tricking the enemy using false identity was a tactic used by both sides during the confused back-and-forth guerrilla war in the South; Tarleton at one point reportedly impersonated a Continental Army cavalry officer in order to escape pursuing Patriots.

The Continental Army's dragoons won their greatest victory at Cowpens. Morgan's army included elements of the 1st and 3rd Continental Dragoons (which at this point had been amalgamated), commanded by Lieutenant Colonel William Washington and supported by a number of state dragoons from North and South Carolina, Virginia, and some Georgians – a cavalry force numbering about 110 once mounted militia were also factored in. This mounted contingent was heavily outnumbered by around 300 dragoons under Tarleton's command. The British and Loyalist dragoons deployed in a standard formation, dividing between a reserve and a group on both flanks. Washington's cavalry, held in the rear, attacked only the right flank of the British line, giving them a localized numerical superiority. After routing the Loyalist cavalry they were able to strike at the flank and rear of the Crown Forces' main line. Tarleton's dragoon reserve refused to charge, and the remains of the Loyalist cavalry were swept aside piecemeal by Washington's dragoons.

The Continental Light Dragoons performed well again at Guilford Courthouse two months later. They counterattacked the 2nd Guards Battalion, producing one of the most protracted engagements between infantry and cavalry of the war; the fight only ended when Cornwallis ordered his artillery to fire indiscriminately into the melee.

Artillery

When the Continental Army was first formed it was severely lacking in artillery, especially the heavy pieces necessary to besiege the British garrison in Boston, which lasted from April 1775 to March 1776. This shortcoming was solved by the efforts and ingenuity of Colonel Henry Knox, a former bookseller and Massachusetts militiaman, who transported 60 tons-worth of captured artillery through the New England wilderness from Fort Ticonderoga to Boston.

Artillery companies and regiments were formed throughout the rebelling colonies between 1775 and 1777. On June 14, 1775, the Regiment of the Train of Artillery in the Massachusetts State Troops was reorganized into the Continental Artillery Regiment, with the Rhode Island Train of Artillery being added to its strength on January 1, 1776. The regiment consisted of 12 companies, each one made up of one captain, one captain-lieutenant, two lieutenants, four sergeants, four corporals, one drummer, one fifer, eight bombardiers, eight gunners, and 32 matrosses. The latter three groups all held the rank of private, but bombardiers and gunners were considered specialist roles and received higher pay (Wright 1983: 53). This regiment was in turn disbanded and other units, such as Lamb's Continental Artillery

At the start of the war British and Patriot artillerists shared many of the same exercises, manuals, and drills. Colonel Henry Knox was particularly important in expanding and standardizing the Continental Army's artillery, and promoted an anti-infantry role on the battlefield that yielded notable results at engagements such as Monmouth Courthouse. (DEA PICTURE LIBRARY/Getty Images)

Regiment and Crane's Continental Artillery Regiment, were amalgamated in 1779 to form a total of four Continental Army artillery regiments.

Like the British, most Continental Army field pieces ranged from 3-, 6-, and 9- to 12-pounders. There were also French 4-pounder cannons available, though a lack of suitable ammunition meant they saw less service. Besides cannons, the Continental Army's arsenal included howitzers and mortars, most commonly 8in and 5.5in respectively. Heavy siege artillery generally consisted of 18- and 24-pounders.

Continental Army artillery did not operate in the ad hoc system of brigades utilized by the British. Lighter pieces were designated battalion guns and attached to the permanent infantry brigades to provide close infantry support, while the heavier artillery was grouped together into larger batteries on the battlefield. Knox in particular emphasized avoiding counterbattery fire in favor of targeting enemy infantry during combat – a decision that drew the approval of Washington at Monmouth Courthouse (Wright 1983: 150).

After an inauspicious start for Patriot artillery at Bunker Hill, where the guns had generally been poorly handled, the Continental Army's artillery quickly developed a reputation for effectiveness, and most likely accounted for more battlefield deaths among Crown Forces than any other service arm. The artillery found prime targets among Hessians packed into the streets of Trenton during the surprise attack on December 26, 1776 before covering the successful withdrawal of Washington's infantry. Nine days later, at Princeton, the close support of battalion guns saved Brigadier General Hugh Mercer's brigade while another battery stymied the attack of Crown forces long enough for Washington to order a counterstrike. Continental Army guns under the command of Captain Alexander Hamilton helped compel the surrender of British forces toward the end of the battle.

Artillery companies attached to infantry brigades helped anchor what could at times be unsteady Continental Army lines. For example, five guns provided the focus for the defense of Birmingham Hill during the battle of Brandywine and were only abandoned after continual Crown Forces sniping had killed the transport horses and a number of the crewmen.

F   **CONTINENTAL ARMY ARTILLERY TACTICS**

Here we see a "grand battery" of six Continental Army iron 6-pounder artillery pieces grouped together at the center of a line of Continental Army infantry. Typically, armies during the American Revolutionary War split their guns between larger, grouped batteries and the smaller "battalion" guns assigned to provide direct support to infantry battalions and brigades.

Projectiles varied depending on the range and target. The British Army's Royal Artillery often sought artillery dominance through counterbattery fire. As the war progressed, however, the Continental Army artillery began to choose enemy infantry as their primary target. At extreme ranges these 6-pounders would utilize solid spherical balls called solid shot or roundshot. Such projectiles skipped across the ground, causing carnage whenever they struck before their kinetic energy was expended. Ideally, such projectiles were used in enfilading fire, in which one ball could cut down a whole rank. At closer ranges gunners would usually switch to canister shot. This involved a metal cylinder, often made from tin, filled with lead or iron balls. The tin would burst upon firing, spreading the balls in a hail from the barrel. Grapeshot provided similar close-range, antipersonnel firepower but used fewer, larger projectiles than canister, packed into a bag, placed on a spherical wooden base, and bound around a wooden rod.

We see enemy infantry in the distance about to enter the battery's effective solid-shot range: 1,500yd (**1**). Farther in, at around 400yd, the gunners will switch to canister or grapeshot, which will give them firepower over a wide arc (**2**). From about 150yd the enemy will be within musket range of the supporting battalions on either side (**3**). Bronze or iron casting meant the ranges on American Revolutionary War artillery pieces varied, with iron guns able to achieve greater distances; for a bronze gun the effective roundshot range was about 1,200yd.

Inset: This limber and caisson – to assist the movement of the gun, and to provide extra ammunition and spare parts respectively – was only the beginning of an artillery train. Battery wagons and mobile forges also necessitated teams of four to six horses.

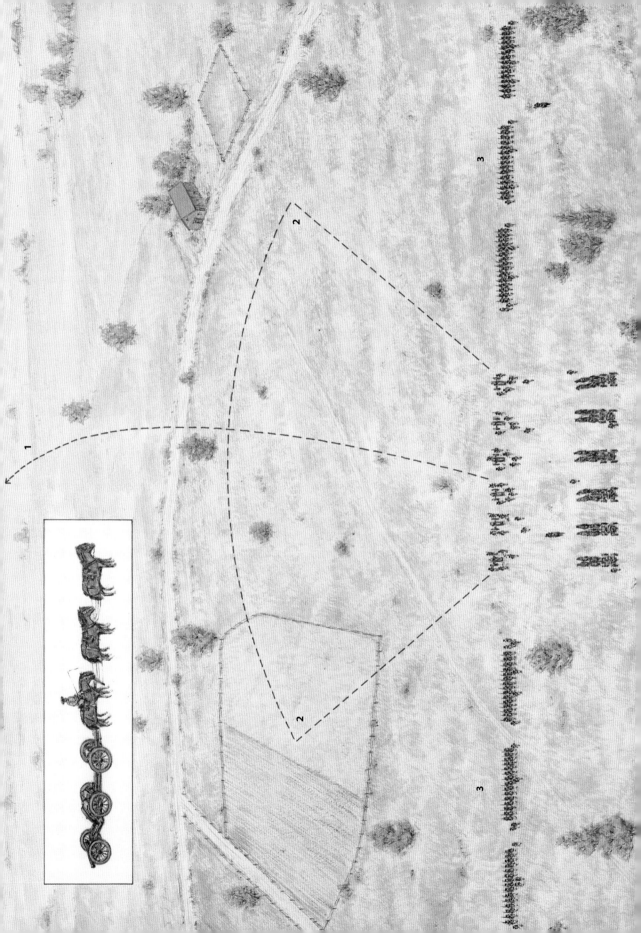

1

2

2

3

3

GERMAN STATE ARMIES

German states had a long history of hiring out soldiers to foreign powers. By the time of the American Revolutionary War, the most prominent state to do so was Hessen-Cassel, which had been providing other states with soldiery for almost a century. Some 10,000 Hessians served under Eugene of Savoy during the War of the Spanish Succession (1701–14) and 6,000 were sent to assist Sweden in the Great Northern War (1700–21). During the War of the Austrian Succession, 6,000 Hessians served on one side of the conflict and 6,000 on the other. In 1762 an army of 12,000 Hessians, supported by militia, was created to be leased out to potential buyers as a single force, essentially a prepackaged army-for-hire (Childs 1999: 64).

Britain was the Landgrave of Hessen-Cassel's most regular customer, hiring Hessian regiments during the War of the Spanish Succession, the 1715 and 1745 Jacobite uprisings, the War of the Austrian Succession, and the Seven Years' War. In 1727 the British government paid the Landgraf for the right to have first pick among states hiring Hessian troops (Childs 1999: 64).

In 1775 Britain faced mobilization problems. Parliament voted to solve these in part by seeking assistance from a number of German states. While the Landgraf of Hessen-Cassel, Friedrich II, provided the largest contingent of troops – estimated between 17,000 and 19,000 – there were five other German states which contributed soldiers to the North American service.

Ruled by Friedrich II's son Wilhelm, Hessen-Hanau, Hessen-Cassel's semi-independent neighbor, supplied one line regiment, one *Jäger* corps, an artillery company, and a regiment of irregular *Freikorps*: a total of 2,422 men. Ruled by Duke Charles I, Braunschweig-Wolfenbüttel provided four line regiments, one grenadier battalion, one light-infantry battalion (this operated as formed support for its *Jäger* company rather than in the broader light-infantry role employed by British light battalions), one dragoon regiment, and one *Jäger* company attached to the light battalion: a total of 5,723 men by the end of the war. Ruled by Margrave Charles Alexander, Ansbach-Bayreuth supplied two line regiments – one from Ansbach and one from Bayreuth, the two later being amalgamated into a single regiment with two battalions – plus one *Jäger* company and a small artillery company consisting of two guns: total forces numbered 2,353 men. Ruled by Prince Friedrich Karl August, Waldeck supplied one line regiment of 1,225 men. Ruled by Prince Frederick Augustus, Anhalt-Zerbst provided one line regiment (including *Pandour* irregulars), one artillery company, and one *Jäger* company: a total of 1,160 men. Finally, Hanover, ruled directly by King George III, also supplied regiments, though they served in Gibraltar, Menorca, and India rather than North America. In total, around 30,000 German soldiers fought as part of the Crown Forces in the Thirteen Colonies and Canada during the American Revolutionary War.

While commentators both at the time and today have described the German soldiers who fought alongside Crown Forces as mercenaries, such a description is not accurate. The soldiers in the state armies of Hessen-Cassel, Braunschweig-Wolfenbüttel, or any of the other powers that gave aid to Great Britain were serving their ruler and their country or principality in the same way as the armies of France and Britain. They were a fully professional military force loyal to their rulers and to their allies.

Hessian organization

Though, like almost all mid-18th-century German militaries, the army of Hessen-Cassel was based upon that of Prussia, Hessen-Cassel actually had the distinction of being the most militarized state in Europe. In 1730, when Hessen-Cassel was not involved in hiring out soldiers or engaged in any wars, 1 in 19 of the Hessen-Cassel populace – over 5.2 percent – were soldiers. This figure rose in times of conflict. Prussia, in contrast, is estimated to have had 4.2 percent of its populace under arms even while at war in the mid-19th century, while a larger state such as Russia had a little over 1 percent under arms (Black 1994: 221). The state also produced its own military materials, from uniforms to weaponry. While the size of the standing army might have been expected to place a strain on the state's economy, the high demand for Hessian regiments ensured it remained prosperous for much of the 18th century.

All Hessian males were required to register for military service from the age of seven. All Hessian men aged between 16 and 30 had to go before an Army board each year and could be eligible for military service. Discipline was stricter than in many 18th-century European armies, but promotion was largely on merit and soldiers could expect better, more regular pay than members of the unskilled laboring and agricultural classes from which the military drew many of its conscripts.

Hessian line regiments were normally organized into two battalions consisting of five regular companies, plus one company of grenadiers. This organization was altered for campaigning in North America: the grenadier companies were detached to form their own battalions, and the line regiments were organized into single battalions. Each of the five regular companies consisted of a captain, two lieutenants, one ensign, three sergeants, one quartermaster sergeant, one provost sergeant, seven corporals, a junior surgeon, three drummers, one clerk, 105 privates, and four officers' servants (Wright 1983: 94–95). While consisting of five companies, each battalion fought in sections of eight platoons. Fire was usually given by divisions consisting of platoon pairings. Regiments billeted by companies, however, which meant it took some time for Hessian battalions to form for battle. The shortcomings of this method of organization were laid bare by Washington's attack on the Hessian garrison at Trenton. Caught by surprise, it took precious time for the three Hessian regiments to stand to and form up.

Tactical limitations in America

Like the Prussians they modeled themselves on, Hessian tactical doctrine called for line formations three ranks deep with the files in close order. The British Army's adoption of two ranks was accepted by Hessian commanders in the field, but Hessian regiments retained the close-order aspect of their traditional formation in spite of the many obstacles presented by the terrain of North American battlefields (Spring 2007: 143).

Tactically, Hessian regiments were also hampered by their speed. The standard marching step Hessian infantry were drilled to was 75 paces per minute (Spring 2007: 147). In North America, British infantry regularly adopted around 120 paces per minute – a considerable divergence in speed (Spring 2007: 145). The natural consequence of this was that Hessian regiments were left behind by advancing British units with some regularity. This disrupted battle lines and left units unsupported, with the Hessians struggling in particular when being harried and picked apart by skirmishing militia and irregulars, such as during the Saratoga campaign.

A Hessian Grenadier.

This caricature of a Hessian grenadier shows a soldier laden down with equipment. While certainly exaggerated, differences in drill did mean that in some engagements Hessian regiments were left behind by their swifter British counterparts. (Anne S.K. Brown Military Collection, Brown University Library)

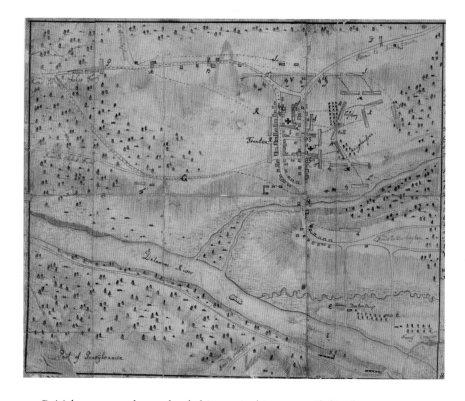

The Patriot victory at Trenton on December 26, 1776, was a vital morale boost for the Continental Army. It also exposed the overconfidence of British strategy, and the tactical shortcomings and lack of preparation among the Hessian forces involved. (Library of Congress)

British commanders solved this tactical incompatibility between Hessian regiments and the rest of the army by employing them in a reserve capacity. Not only did this mean the Hessians were not required to keep up with the leading edge of an attack, but their three-rank, closed-files formation also provided stability and a rallying point should British forces be repulsed. Indeed, there were instances when the close-order formation used by Hessian regiments was highly effective, providing a decisive mass of firepower. During the capture of Savannah it was noted that while British troops in open order struggled to bring enough muskets to bear to break the Patriots, the arrival of the Hessian musketeer regiment von Trümbach, tightly ranked, delivered volleys of musket fire that overwhelmed the Patriots (Spring 2007: 213). Other tactical roles requiring less mobility could also be readily filled by the Hessians: at both Long Island and Brandywine, German troops were used as diversionary and pinning forces, holding the attention of the enemy while wide flanking movements by British regulars turned and collapsed the Continental Army's defenses.

Petitions were made to Friedrich II to allow his forces to adopt the tactical doctrines used by other Crown Forces, specifically open order and an emphasis on rapid advances and the bayonet. The Landgraf refused, however, also stipulating that his regiments were not to make any uniform modifications to accommodate campaigning in North America – something which the British did regularly (Spring 2007: 147–48). While usually forming in two ranks, the Hessian regiments employed what British sergeant Roger Lamb described at Guilford Courthouse as "firm and compact order" (Lamb 1809: 354).

Despite this there were instances of Hessian tactical innovation in the field. Besides the preexisting dedicated *Jäger* units, volunteers were sometimes drawn from line regiments to serve as *chasseurs* or light infantry. At one point they formed a composite battalion under Captain George Hanger, acting in the same manner as the British grenadier and light-infantry battalions (Atwood 1980: 96). Also – at least when first deployed to America – Hessian troops made use of the same light, rapid assault tactics utilized by the British. At the engagement at Flatbush Pass during the battle of Long Island, the Hessian advance was spearheaded by *Jäger* and skirmishing grenadiers and closely supported by 3-pounder artillery. The main force that followed in their wake likewise employed open order to traverse the woodland through which they found themselves advancing, and then attacked the Patriot forces with the bayonet, easily routing them (Atwood 1980: 68). The rapidity of their victory appears to have lulled some Hessians into underestimating the Patriots, however, a mistake they would pay for dearly at Trenton three months later. Generally, Hessian officers seem to have believed that their *Jäger* and *chasseur* companies provided sufficient tactical flexibility for fighting in North America, without permanently adopting the open order (Atwood 1980: 83).

Other German states

The Braunschweig-Wolfenbüttel and Hessen-Hanau regiments each had a single battalion of five line companies and one grenadier company; the Braunschweig-Wolfenbüttel grenadier companies were detached to form a composite battalion, while the Hessen-Hanau grenadier companies remained with their parent regiment. As with the Hessians, however, the line company was not the combat unit – that consisted of the battalion being divided into two wings, each consisting of two divisions, and each division divided into two platoons, which acted as the basis for firing groupings, usually by division.

Not all German states were as rigid in their tactical application as the Hessians. The regiments sent by Braunschweig-Wolfenbüttel agreed to adopt two ranks and open order as part of Burgoyne's June 1777 expedition from Quebec. Burgoyne stressed that he expected his German and British infantry to be able to act in concert while maneuvering at speed (Spring 2007: 148). The commander of the German forces, Major-General Friedrich Adolf Riedesel, learned the advantage of the American method of fighting in open order, and issued orders to his officers to drill his men in this new system, "thus adding a useful lesson to the strict German discipline" (Eelking 1893: 129). Riedesel worked hard to familiarize his German troops with North American warfare, and his instruction "urges the necessity of instructing them to fight in open order, to secure the shelter of trees or cover of any kind, and only to fire from that position, except when meeting the enemy in the open, then to fire and attack at once with the bayonet, in close order" (Eelking 1893: 272–73). Riedesel also described drilling his troops in the use of firepower during irregular fighting, emphasizing the degree to which Braunschweig-Wolfenbüttel soldiers tried to adapt to North American warfare:

> As soon as the first line has jumped into the supposed ditch, the command "fire" is given, when the first line fires, reloads its guns, gets up out of the ditch, and hides behind a tree, rock, shrub or whatever is at hand, at the same time firing off four cartridges in such a manner that the line is kept as straight as possible. As soon as the first line has fired off the four cartridges, the second line advances and fires off the same number in the same manner. While this is taking place, the woods have been thoroughly ransacked by the sharp shooters who have thus become familiar with every part of it. (Quoted in Stone 1868: 64)

Waldeck's regiment likewise utilized two ranks and open order. From 1755 Waldeck had operated an extensive form of conscription, but at first only volunteers were called upon to serve in America. Soldiers from two Waldeck regiments in the Netherlands were transferred into a third regiment, with numbers having to be supplemented by recruiting parties in other Germanic states. The regiment arrived in America in October 1776 and was engaged at Long Island, White Plains, and Fort Washington. In 1778 the Waldeckers were transported to British-held Florida, where they suffered heavy casualties (largely from disease) while fighting the Spanish. The survivors returned to New York in 1781, where they remained until the end of the war.

The final German state to send a contingent to North America, Anhalt-Zerbst, differed from the other five insomuch as the soldiers' drill, doctrines, and uniform regulations were not based on those of Prussia, but the other great German-speaking power, Austria. The Princess of Anhalt's Regiment, a force of two battalions which included many recruits from other German states, was raised and arrived in Canada in 1778, where it garrisoned Quebec. Part of this force, described as *Pandour* irregulars, was sent to New York in 1780, though whether these troops served in a light-infantry capacity is a moot point, as the regiment did not see serious action before the end of the war.

Cavalry

Only a single dedicated regiment of German cavalry was deployed to North America, namely the Braunschweig-Wolfenbüttel dragoon regiment Prinz Ludwig. Trained in shock tactics and equipped with the *Pallasch* (broadsword), they had the potential to be the heaviest cavalry regiment on the North American continent. Unfortunately, they ultimately suffered one of the worst fates of any cavalry regiment of the war: they arrived in North America without mounts, and were never re-equipped. They consequently served as infantry, replacing their boots and breeches with gaitered trousers made from distinctive blue-and-white striped bed ticking, though it seems they chose to keep their heavy broadswords – at least in their campaign baggage. During the Saratoga campaign some were equipped with horses and used as scouts and videttes, but most remained on foot. Their commander, Lieutenant Colonel Friedrich Baum, was sent with the regiment to Bennington, partly to acquire horses. Baum's men were attacked by a large force of Patriot militia there on August 16, 1777. After their Loyalist militia and Native American allies were killed, routed, or captured, the Braunschweig-Wolfenbüttel dragoons fought on from a small hilltop redoubt. Their gunpowder wagon was destroyed, and after running out of ammunition they decided to attempt to break out on foot. They conducted a charge downhill with drawn swords, but most of them, including Baum, were shot down. The regiment's survivors were reconfigured in Canada, but saw little further service.

Artillery

Hessen-Cassel and Hessen-Hanau both provided artillery companies for service in America, with Ansbach-Bayreuth also fielding two cannons as close support for what became the state's sole two-battalion regiment in America. Regardless of which state they hailed from, the German artillery consisted of lighter field pieces, mostly 3- and 6-pounders; there were no heavy siege-artillery contingents.

The three Hessian artillery companies had been recruited specifically for the deployment to North America. Volunteers were difficult to find, however, so requests were made to draft in dragoons (Atwood 1980: 45). Six guns were lost during the disaster at Trenton, though many of the gunners escaped capture by fleeing the battle early.

The sole Hessen-Hanau artillery company saw service with Burgoyne's expedition from Canada. Commanded by Captain George Pausch, they spent time operating on gunboats during the battle of Valcour Island, a naval engagement conducted on Lake Champlain on October 11, 1776. At Saratoga they employed one group of four 6-pounders and a second group consisting of two 6-pounders and two 3-pounders, all British-supplied. The four light guns acted as battalion support for the Braunschweig-Wolfenbüttel grenadier regiment von Breymann and the light-infantry battalion von Barner. Indeed, close support was the most regular role of German field guns, an aspect emphasized by Pausch's service at Freeman's Farm. The German artillery supported their infantry with grapeshot before switching to roundshot that they expertly fired over the heads of the infantry once their support units charged, thus helping break the Patriot onslaught. Several weeks later, on October 7, 1777, the Hessen-Hanau gunners performed the same duties at the battle of Bemis Heights, during which they were engaged for so long that their gun barrels began to glow red-hot. Patriot pressure forced them to relocate the artillery on two occasions during the battle, until most of the limber horses were killed. Refusing to abandon the regiments his guns were supporting, Pausch's artillery was finally overrun.

Jäger

Jäger were light infantrymen that had been employed by various German states, most notably Prussia, since the Seven Years' War. Armed with rifles and typically recruited from huntsmen, foresters, and gamekeepers, the *Jäger* companies sent to North America were considered an elite skirmishing force.

The *Feldjäger* corps, as it became, was originally comprised of two companies of rifle-armed soldiers from Hessen-Cassel that formed part of the Hessian contingent sent to America in 1776. A year later, three more foot companies and one mounted company were added to the force, giving it a total strength of around 500 men. At full combat strength a *Jäger* company consisted of four commissioned officers, 16 non-commissioned officers, and 105 men. Hessen-Hanau, Braunschweig-Wolfenbüttel, and Ansbach-Bayreuth all provided their own *Jäger* companies, very similar in appearance to those of Hessen-Cassel, with green coats and red facings in the Prussian style. The Hessen-Hanau and Braunschweig-Wolfenbüttel *Jäger* were deployed to Canada and were captured at Saratoga, while the Ansbach-Bayreuth *Jäger* were amalgamated with the Hessen-Cassel corps serving with the main British field army under Howe. In 1777 the coats of the Hessians, worn out by heavy campaigning, were replaced with green Provincials coats given to the corps by Cornwallis.

Jäger used various similar models of short German hunting rifles; those used by the Hessian contingent were made at the Pistor Manufactory at Schmalkalden. These weapons allowed the *Jäger* to compete effectively with rifle-armed Patriots, be they Continental Army soldiers or militia. They were therefore utilized as an advanced skirmishing and screening force by Crown Forces commanders. For example, Captain Johann Ewald, who

was to rise to prominence as perhaps the best light-infantry commander among Crown Forces during the war, led the vanguard of the flanking force at Brandywine, his *Jäger* supported by British light-infantry companies (Spring 2007: 87). The two British columns that attacked the Patriots at White Plains were both headed by a *Jäger* company which first drove off enemy skirmishers and then engaged in the *Jäger*'s most typical style of warfare in difficult terrain against Patriot riflemen, advancing under heavy cannon fire through swamps and ravines before successfully routing the enemy (Ewald 1979: 13).

Working closely with regular infantry was a key tactical facet of the *Feldjäger* corps, and the area in which they saw greatest success. As previously mentioned, *Jäger* and grenadiers in loose order advanced in the vanguard together at Flatbush Pass, and repeated the same feat crossing the Schuylkill River on December 11, 1777. Indeed, grenadiers appear to have operated alongside the *Jäger* as frequently as light infantry in the campaigns of 1776 and 1777. While the *Jäger* were able to ward off Patriot riflemen and skirmishers, the grenadiers could maintain pace with them in their own newly adopted loose formation, but with the potential to become a formed, bayonet-wielding body of troops if they were seriously threatened.

British officers were near-universal in their praise of the skirmishing capabilities of the *Jäger*. Cornwallis commented that one *Jäger* was the equivalent of ten Patriot soldiers (Spring 2007: 31). An anonymous officer who wrote to the *London Chronicle* observed that "nothing could behave better than the Hessians, and particularly their Jägers, or riflemen, who are much superior to those of the rebels as it is possible to imagine" (Dick 1776: 89). Against unsteady troops the *Jäger* were even capable of mounting assaults, armed with the short swords they utilized for want of *Hirschfänger* ("deer catcher") bayonets. At Germantown an exposed force of *Jäger* counterattacked Patriot militia holding a bridge, charging them and driving them from the battlefield.

Jäger companies also served as mounted troops on occasions when there were sufficient horses. They did so not as makeshift cavalry, but in the traditional dragoon role, as mounted infantry who would use their horses' speed to maneuver rapidly, then dismount and engage in their usual skirmish order. However, their unsuitability in a cavalry role was exposed when Continental Army dragoons ambushed and routed both mounted and foot *Jäger* near Dobbs Ferry on September 30, 1778.

G **HESSIANS ADVANCE AT FLATBUSH PASS**
At the battle of Long Island on August 27, 1776, Hessian forces demonstrate to hold the attention of the Patriots while the main British army outflanks them. Ordered to advance at the height of the battle, the Hessians approach a forest in Flatbush Pass in a manner far removed from the stereotypical view of the inflexible "Prussian drill." Their advance is preceded by parties of *Jäger* (**1**) supported by grenadiers also in loose skirmish formation (**2**). The presence of the grenadiers allows the *Jäger* to form a line of battle quickly should they meet with formed enemy resistance or cavalry, offering the light troops greater security. Also supporting the advance of the skirmishers are light 3-pounder artillery pieces (**3**), while some of the men are armed with *amusettes*.

Behind this powerful skirmish screen the main battalions advance (**4**). Upon reaching the woods they detached picked men who pushed on in open order, further guarding the main line from the threat of being caught up in irregular combat among the trees. By the time the Hessian forces advanced at Flatbush Pass the Patriot forces were largely broken, and the Hessians met only light resistance.

Inset: *Jäger* utilizing an *amusette*. These were essentially scaled-up muskets of a much larger caliber and could offer support for light-infantry units that did not want to be slowed by the use of light cannons.

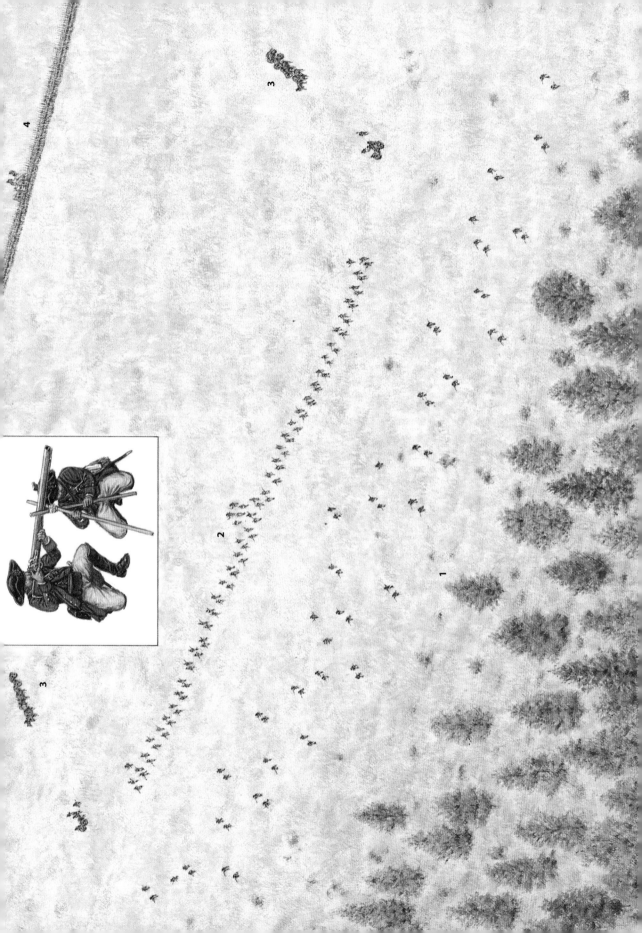

THE FRENCH ARMY

The commander of the major French expedition to America in 1780, the Comte de Rochambeau, was somewhat dissatisfied by what could be perceived to be a lack of progress by French tacticians during the 1770s. He believed that well-regulated firepower had a greater part to play than some assault-minded French generals allowed for. (Fine Art Images/Heritage Images/Getty Images)

For much of the 17th and early 18th centuries, France's standing army was considered the best in Europe. Near-total defeat in the Seven Years' War came as a severe shock, however, leading to a series of reforms throughout the French military that were initially spearheaded by Étienne François, duc de Choiseul. A 1764 *Ordonnance du Roi* (royal order) began to modernize French military regulations, and tactical doctrines followed. This culminated in the 1776 and 1779 *Règlements* (regulations), which partly emphasized firepower based on the Prussian model: three-rank lines for delivery of massed musketry, the use of open columns for maneuver, and the close, regimented supervision of soldiers by their officers.

A range of other reforms updated the French Army. Uniforms and equipment became more standardized. The artillery system was completely overhauled. A number of military schools were founded to give practical education to aspiring officers. Colonels deemed surplus were dismissed from the oversized officer corps. On March 25, 1776, an edict was issued that, among other changes, ended the use of corporal punishment on regular soldiers and phased out the purchasing of commissions, with officers henceforth chosen from the graduates of the new military schools instead (Abel 2016: 109–12). The flurry of reforms met resistance from more conservative members of the French Army and court: in 1781, for example, a reactionary royal order ensured that only those of aristocratic lineage could be granted officers' commissions. Despite this, the changes implemented since the early 1760s meant that by the outbreak of the American Revolutionary War the French military was on the cusp of becoming Europe's foremost land force once more.

In 1770 Jacques Antoine Hippolyte, Comte de Guibert, published his *Essai général de tactique*. A French Army officer and leading military theorist, Guibert had already advised the French War Ministry in 1766 about the potential of the *ordre mixte*, a tactical concept which included infantry utilized in both line and column and closely supported by artillery (Wright 1983: 139). In the wake of the Seven Years' War, debate had raged in France between the proponents of the *ordre profond* and the *ordre mince*. Guibert's system appeared to offer an ideal compromise, but was attacked by other theorists, such as François-Jean de Mensil-Durand in his 1774 *Fragments de tactique*. The benefits of combining formations and the potential inherent in such flexibility, while not initially adopted by the French military, not only influenced French thinking but also the formation of a tactical doctrine by the Continental Army, with soldiers encouraged to become proficient in a wider range of tactical maneuvers.

With the outbreak of war between Britain and France in 1778, the French Army conducted a series of military maneuvers at Vaussieux in Normandy, as well as in Brittany. Besides threatening Britain's security through their presence on the Channel coast, these war games put the developments of the past decade to the test in a training environment. The *ordre profond* and the *ordre mince* were employed against one another. Led by the future commander of the French expedition to North America, Jean-Baptiste Donatien de Vimeur, Comte de Rochambeau, a brigade utilizing the thinner lines and greater maneuverability of the *ordre mince* managed to defeat a much larger force employing the *ordre profond*. Similar exercises were repeated, with an increased use of skirmishers giving the more unwieldy

columns of the *ordre profond* better protection. The training, while slowly pushing theorists toward the compromise of the *ordre mixte*, had the more immediate effect of readying French forces for their campaigns against Britain across the globe (Abel 2016: 128–32).

In 1776, as part of the ongoing French Army reforms, regiments were reduced from four battalions to two. In keeping with most European militaries (but unlike the British), a regiment's twin battalions campaigned and were deployed together on the battlefield. Both battalions had four fusilier (center) companies, a grenadier company, and a *chasseur* (light infantry) company. The fusilier and *chasseur* companies each consisted of one captain, one first lieutenant, one second lieutenant, two sub-lieutenants, one sergeant major, one quartermaster sergeant, five sergeants, ten corporals, one gentleman-cadet, one surgeon's assistant, 144 privates, and two drummers. Grenadier companies consisted of one captain, one second captain, one first lieutenant, one second lieutenant, two sub-lieutenants, one sergeant major, one quartermaster sergeant, four sergeants, eight corporals, one gentleman-cadet, one surgeon's assistant, 84 privates, and two drummers. Total strength for a two-battalion regiment, including its command staff and an auxiliary recruit company, therefore stood at 1,990 officers and men. As with all other armies involved in the American Revolutionary War, however, the realities of deployment and combat meant that this ideal figure was almost never reached, and the regiments that took to the field were usually far smaller (Chartrand 1991: 9).

On July 3–4, 1779, French forces stormed the British defenses on Hospital Hill, Grenada. In doing so they displayed the effective us of diversionary tactics and assault columns, taking the works with minimal loss. (DEA/M. SEEMULLER/Getty Images)

In 1778 the French Army's strength stood at around 236,000 men, not to mention the 75,000 militiamen who guarded France's coasts and, in some cases, were used to supplement the regular regiments (Chartrand 1991: 10). French military forces engaged Britain not only in the closing years of the war in North America but, over a period of six years in the Caribbean, in the Channel, in the Mediterranean, and in India. Without the massive contribution by France, the victory of the United States would have been almost impossible.

Assault columns

While the *ordre mince* – at its core, the reliance on linear, firepower tactics – had ostensibly won the post-Seven Years' War debate as regards future French tactics, the realities of the American Revolutionary War saw the frequent use of French columns as an offensive tool. Both in North America and the Caribbean, French forces were frequently required to attack defended positions, often as part of siege operations. Rochambeau, despite being a firm adherent of the *ordre mince*, never got the tactical opportunity to test his army in line against a massed force of British regulars.

Siege warfare saw the French assault column meet with only limited success over the course of the war. Over 3,000 French troops composed the force that laid siege to Savannah in September–October 1779, with both French and Patriot troops falling under the overall command of the French Admiral Charles Hector, Comte d'Estaing. On October 9, French infantry contributed two columns to the force that attacked the town's fortifications at the Spring Hill redoubt. The attack was initially confounded by fog and marshy ground, and suffered from the fire of rifle-armed Loyalist militia. The redoubt was heavily defended primarily by Loyalists and Scots of the 71st Regiment of Foot, and the assault was repulsed with great loss. Poor communication between French and American commanders, both prior to and during combat, had hampered the assault from the start.

Worse was to come two months later at Vigie Peninsula on Saint Lucia, as four columns of French troops were defeated by British heavy artillery and infantry that were veterans of the fighting in North America. In both battles the French columns struggled with difficult terrain and lacked adequate support from either artillery or infantry deployed in line. The columns' unwieldy, cumbersome formation made them optimal targets for enemy cannon fire, and they struggled to clear away skirmishers used to fighting Patriot irregulars and militia. Because of these factors the column's greatest strength – a dense mass of men that could be used for shock assault – could not be delivered to its target.

OPPOSITE
Marie-Joseph Paul Yves Roch Gilbert du Motier, Marquis de La Fayette – known as Lafayette to his American contemporaries – commanded Patriot troops at Yorktown and elsewhere. He is pictured here with James Armistead, a double agent who gathered valuable intelligence for the Patriot cause. (Interim Archives/ Getty Images)

French columns enjoyed greater success elsewhere. On July 3–4, 1779, d'Estaing successfully stormed British defenses on Hospital Hill, on the Caribbean island of Grenada. Three columns of French infantry, each 300 strong, were formed as the sun set on July 3. A fourth group of men conducted a noisy demonstration before the British positions while the columns swept up the steep flanks of the hillside under the cover of darkness. The British were routed almost immediately, and the last of the island's defenders surrendered that same day. The use of a covered approach and a decoy had allowed the French columns to be delivered effectively, with the tactic of sudden, overwhelming force sufficient to break the morale of the British defenders.

The crowning achievement of a French column, at least symbolically, was at the siege of Yorktown in September–October 1781. On October 14, with a large demonstration against the nearby British defenses occupying the attention of the enemy, French infantry stormed Redoubt 9, once more successfully using speed and the onset of darkness to overrun the heavily outnumbered defenders. At the same time Continental Army light infantry stormed Redoubt 10, with both groups relying on the bayonet and, at least in the case of the French, hand grenades. Hospital Hill and Yorktown both demonstrated that with the effective use of misdirection, the cover of darkness, and speed, the assault column could be highly effective.

Cavalry

Like the British and German forces involved in the American Revolutionary War, the French Army sent comparatively little in the way of cavalry to the American theaters. A small force of dragoons from the regiments Condé and Belsunce had been deployed to Saint-Dominigue on the Caribbean island of Hispaniola (modern-day Haiti and the Dominican Republic) and were part of the Franco-Patriot army that unsuccessfully besieged Savannah. They served as scouts and videttes, and did not see action as a formed force.

H **ASSAULT COLUMNS IN SIEGE WARFARE**
On the evening of October 14, 1781, French and Patriot forces employed two assault columns to mount a simultaneous attack on two British redoubts protecting the final approaches to Yorktown. Here we see two such assault columns initially formed up behind the siege lines prior to advancing. As at Yorktown, both the French (**1**) and Patriot (**2**) formations shown here are configured to apply a substantial body of men over a relatively small frontage in an effort to punch through the enemy's defenses.

Attack columns such as these differed from columns formed to facilitate speed of movement on the battlefield; typically, a column of maneuver would consist of a single battalion or brigade, and would have a narrow frontage and greater depth. Prior to engaging, the companies forming the column would wheel out into a line, usually of two ranks. Attack columns, however, utilized a wider frontage to provide some degree of return fire and stop the formation from being enveloped; its frontage often consisted of two companies, with a battalion usually forming a total of six to eight ranks deep. Throughout the American Revolutionary War such formations were typically employed only during attacks on fortified positions.

The Patriot column that stormed Redoubt 10 at Yorktown consisted of 400 light infantrymen. Patriot light infantry had previous experience in such attacks; it was the light-infantry companies which had captured the British-held fort at Stony Point on July 16, 1779, attacking as they did at Yorktown, with unloaded muskets and fixed bayonets. The battalions used at Yorktown – those of Lieutenant Colonel Jean-Joseph Sourbader de Gimat and Lieutenant Colonel Alexander Hamilton, with a flanking detachment under Lieutenant Colonel Henry Laurens – were spearheaded by a force of sappers and volunteers (not shown here) to cut through the abatis (a defensive obstruction made up of felled trees). The French column attacking Redoubt 9 consisted primarily of 400 grenadiers and *chasseurs* from the Gâtinais and Royal Deux-Ponts regiments. During the assault the Patriot light infantry refused to wait for their sappers to clear the obstructions before Redoubt 10, preferring to rush through sections of abatis that had been damaged by artillery fire.

Inset: Grenadiers of the Gâtinais regiment. *Chasseurs* and grenadiers led the French assault at Yorktown; while grenadiers rarely actually used grenades in the 18th century, such explosives were employed at Yorktown to blast apart tightly packed defenders.

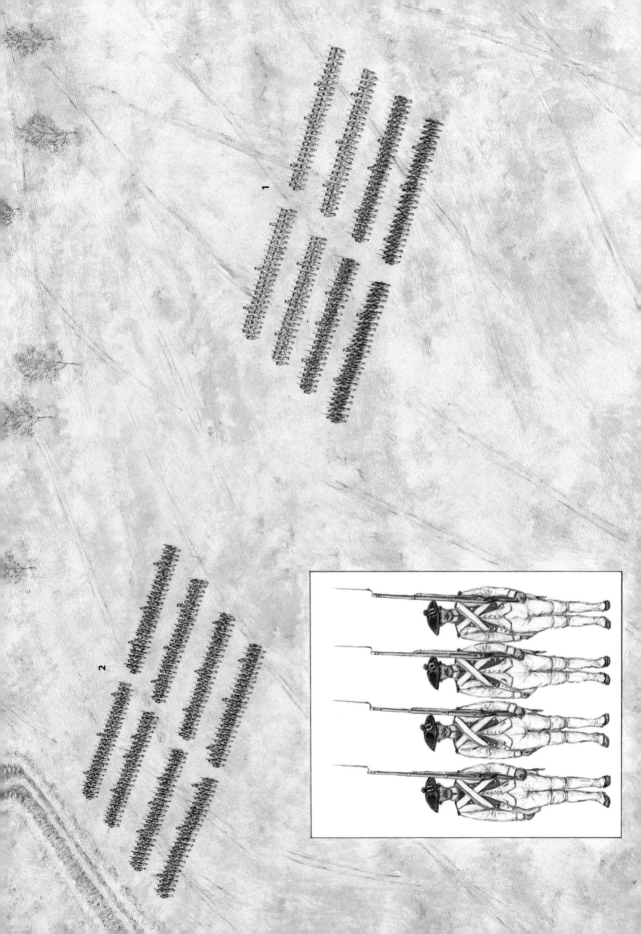

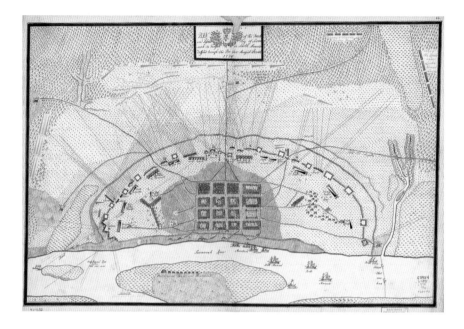

The largest French deployment of horsemen came in the form of Lauzan's Legion, part of Rochambeau's L'Expédition Particulière (The Special Expedition) to North America. In 1778 the creation of eight legions of mixed cavalry and infantry from a force of foreign volunteers had been authorized by the French Navy, the department responsible for France's colonial and overseas troops. Only three of these legions were formed, however, and most of their constituent companies were deployed to Senegal and the West Indies. One, the 2e Légion des Volontaires Étrangers de la Marine, later known as the Légion des Volontaires Étrangers de Lauzun, was assigned in part to Rochambeau's army.

The legion arrived in North America without any horses. Mounts acquired from Pennsylvania were used to equip two squadrons of light cavalry. Lauzan's riders were uniformed in the Hungarian style, as hussars, and equipped with lances. They fulfilled important but near-bloodless duties in providing an advance guard for the advancing Franco-Patriot army, until their only major combat encounter of the war at Gloucester Point on October 3, 1781. While the main British army in the South was being besieged at nearby Yorktown, Lauzun's cavalry engaged British Legion dragoons commanded by Tarleton. The Loyalist dragoons found themselves initially hemmed in at a narrow lane and unable to combat the French lances. They were driven back and Tarleton was unhorsed and almost captured. A counterattack was also defeated by the French, who in turn fell back from a detachment of the 23rd Regiment of Foot which had come up in Tarleton's support. The engagement illustrated the back-and-forth nature of the small-scale actions that characterized instances of cavalry versus cavalry during the American Revolutionary War, and their unwillingness to attempt to engage formed and prepared infantry. Simply put, mounted troops were usually too few in number to be regularly risked in general actions.

Artillery

France had traditionally been a leader in European artillery tactics and organization. The Seven Years' War dented French prestige, however, especially in light of the new methods of artillery usage that had been developed by Prussia and Austria. France responded with a new system conceived of largely by Lieutenant General Jean Baptiste Vaquette de Gribeauval who, from 1764, was France's Inspector of Artillery. In the immediate aftermath of the Seven Years' War France was still using the 1732 Vallière system, first developed by Jean-Florent de Vallière. While effective in siege operations, the Vallière system lacked clear distinctions between field and siege guns and had no standardization in terms of limbers, caissons, and other modes of transport and supply. Gribeauval had spent time studying both the Prussian and Austrian artillery prior to and during the Seven Years' War and believed the Vallière system to be outdated. Vallière's son, Joseph Florent, had been promoted to the rank of Commander of the Battalions and Schools of the Artillery in 1747 and campaigned for his father's system to remain the standard practice of the French artillery. This resulted in a power struggle between two factions, Vallière's reds and Gribeauval's blues, so named after the respective proposed colors of the artillery gunners' uniforms.

Gribeauval's ideas gradually won out and a wide-ranging series of reforms, technological advancements, and standardizations were implemented from the mid-1760s through the mid-1770s. New guns had shorter, thinner barrels, while their carriages were built to be lighter, almost halving their overall weight. Innovations such as rear sights, a standard elevating screw, and a searcher to find any possible defects within barrel bores after repeated firings led to improvements in both accuracy and reliability. Tactical maneuverability and flexibility was increased with the standard introduction of the *bricole*, a drag rope secured around an artillerist with a leather shoulder strap, hooked to a gun's axles and along the side of its carriage to allow soldiers to drag the piece in the absence of horses; the *prolonge*, a length of rope used to redeploy the gun quickly without limbering it, by dragging the trail and helping the piece over difficult terrain using the handspike; and iron axles for carriages and other transportation vehicles. Ammunition was also improved, with better quality gunpowder, vent-prickers to pierce the bags used for powder charges, and a quick-match tube made from tin, a reed, or a quill, which improved ignition compared to the old slow match (Weigley 1991: 272).

Though Gribeauval did not invent most of these innovations himself, he was responsible for collating the best practices from across Europe and streamlining them into his new system. Gunnery schools were established to teach and train artillerists in the French military, returning France's gunners to the forefront of European artillery in both practice and theory. In general, French tactical doctrine on the use of artillery shifted from emphasizing heavy guns and siege operations to highlighting the importance of lighter, maneuverable field pieces used in close support with infantry. Like Knox's Continental Army artillerists, theorists such as Guibert advised a more antipersonnel role, targeting enemy infantry rather than engaging in long-range, often inconclusive counterbattery duels with opposing artillery.

Gribeauval's system was still being refined as the American Revolutionary War broke out, and the 200-odd guns supplied to the rebelling colonists by France were all older Vallière models. It is likely, however, that the French expeditionary force sent to America in 1780 included Gribeauval guns, especially in its heavy siege train. At Yorktown these pieces, and the scientific expertise of French military engineers, made a vital contribution to the effective conduct of the siege.

BIBLIOGRAPHY

Abel, Jonathan (2016). *Guibert: Father of Napoleon's Grande Armée.* Norman, OK: University of Oklahoma Press.

Atwood, Rodney (1980). *The Hessians: Mercenaries from Hessen-Kassel in the American Revolution.* Cambridge: Cambridge University Press.

Black, Jeremy (1994). *European Warfare: 1660–1815.* London: UCL Press.

Blackmore, David (2014). *Destructive and Formidable: British Infantry Firepower 1642–1765.* London: Frontline Books.

Campbell, Archibald, ed. Colin Campbell (1891). *Journal of an expedition against the rebels of Georgia in North America under the orders of Archibald Campbell Esquire Lieut. Col. of His Majesty's 71st Regimt. 1778.* Darien, GA: Ashantilly.

Chartrand, René (1991). *The French Army in the American War of Independence.* Men-at Arms 244. Oxford: Osprey Publishing.

Childs, John (1999). "The Army and the State in Britain and Germany during the Eighteenth Century," in John Childs & Eckhardt Hellmuth, eds, *Rethinking Leviathan: The Eighteenth-century State in Britain and Germany.* Oxford: Oxford University Press: 53–70.

Dean, Charles, Samuel A. Green, & Charles C. Smith (1873). *Proceedings of the Massachusetts Historical Society.* Boston, MA: The Society.

Dick, Robert (1776). *The North-British intelligencer: or Constitutional Miscellany.* Volume I. Edinburgh: William Auld.

Downman, Francis, ed. F.A. Whinyates (1898). *The Services of Lieut.-Colonel Francis Downman, R.A. in France, North America, and the West Indies, Between the Years 1758 and 1784.* Woolwich: The Royal Artillery Institution.

Eelking, Max von (1893). *The German Allied Troops in the North American War of Independence.* Albany, NY: Joel Munsell's Sons.

Eid, Leroy V. (1988). "A King of Running Fight: Indian Battlefield Tactics in the Late Eighteenth Century," *Western Pennsylvania Historical Magazine* 71: 147–72.

Ewald, Johann, trans. Joseph P. Tustin (1979). *Diary of the American War: A Hessian Journal.* New Haven, CT: Yale University Press.

Graham, William A. (1904). *General Joseph Graham and His Papers on North Carolina Revolutionary History.* Raleigh, NC: Edwards & Broughton.

Greene, George Washington (1867). *The Life of Nathanael Greene, Major-General in the Army of the Revolution, Volume 2.* Bedford, MA: Applewood Books.

Harvey, Edward (1776). *The Manual Exercise as Ordered by His Majesty in the Year 1764.* Philadelphia, PA: J. Humphreys, R. Bell, R. Aitken.

Hoock, Holger (2017). *Scars of Independence: America's Violent Birth.* New York, NY: Crown Publishing.

Hunt, Gaillard (1892). *Fragments of Revolutionary War History.* Brooklyn, NY: Historical Printing Club.

Lamb, Roger (1809). *An Original and Authentic Journal of Occurrences During the Late American War from its Commencement to the Year 1783.* Dublin: Wilkinson & Courtney.

Lender, Mark Edward & Garry Wheeler Stone (2016). *Fatal Sunday: George Washington, the Monmouth Campaign, and the Politics of Battle*. Norman, OK: University of Oklahoma Press.

Mackenzie, Frederick (1787). *Strictures on Lt. Col. Tarleton's History of the Campaigns of 1780 and 1781 in the Southern Provinces of North America*. London: Jameson, Faulder, Egerton, & Sewell.

Muhlenberg, Henry Augustus (1849). *The Life of Major-General Peter Muhlenberg: Of the Revolutionary Army*. Philadelphia, PA: Carey & Hart.

Spring, Matthew H. (2007). *With Zeal and With Bayonets Only: The British Army on Campaign in North America, 1775–1784*. Norman, OK: University of Oklahoma Press.

Steuben, Wilhelm Frederick von (1794). *Regulations for the Order and Discipline of the Troops of the United States*. Boston, MA: I. Thomas & E.T. Andrews.

Stone, William L. (1868). *Memoirs and Letters and Journals, of Major General Riedesel, During His Residence in America, Volume 1*. Albany, NY: J. Munsell.

Wayne, Anthony (1893). "Camp Near Pauling Mill," in Charles J. Stille, ed., *Major-General Anthony Wayne and the Pennsylvania Line of the Continental Army*. Philadelphia, PA: J.B. Lippincott Co.: 96.

Weigley, Russel Frank (1991). *The Age of Battles: The Quest for Decisive Warfare from Breitenfeld to Waterloo*. Bloomington & Indianapolis, IN: Indiana University Press.

Wright, Robert K. (1983). *The Continental Army*. Washington, DC: Center of Military History.

This satirical piece shows British armies entrapped in the coils of a rattlesnake, here a representation of the rebelling colonists. The loss of field armies at the battle of Saratoga and the siege of Yorktown ultimately broke British efforts in the Thirteen Colonies and validated the long-term strategies of the likes of Washington. (Encyclopaedia Britannica/Getty Images)

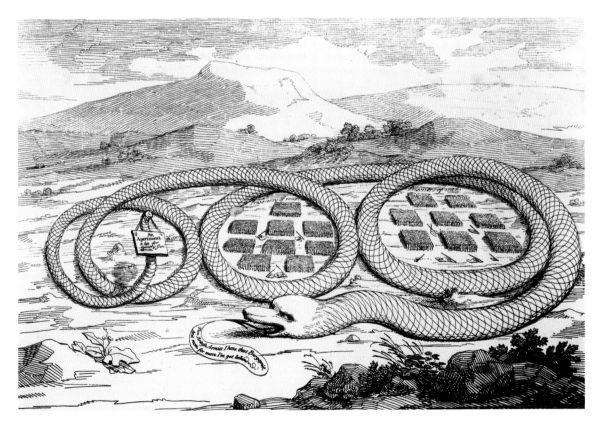

INDEX

References to illustrations are shown in **bold**. Plates are shown with page locators in brackets.

artillery forces: (GB) 6, 18–20, **19**, 43, 44, 56; (US) **4**, 40, 41, 42, **42**, 43–44, **43**, **F(45)**; (Ger) 46, 50, 51; (Fr) 54, 61
artillery pieces: (GB) 16, 18–19, 20, 44, 50, 56; (US) 16, 42, **42**, 43, **43**, 44, **F(45)**; (Ger) 46, 49, 50, 51, 52, **G(53)**; (Fr) 61
assault/attack columns (Fr) 56, 58, **H(59)**

Baylor, Col. George 14, 40
bayonets, use of: (GB) 12–13, 24, 34, 36, 38; (US) 13, 24, 30, 32, 35, 36, **36**, 58; (Ger) 49, 52
Bemis Heights, battle of (1777) 51
Bennington, attack at (1777) 50
Boston, retreat to (1775) 13, **13**, 19, 37
Bound Brook, battle of (1777) 40
Brandywine, battle of (1777) 14, 18, 19, 27, 31, 44, 48, 52
British Army formations/tactics
alternate-fire systems 10–11
columns from battalions 7
flank companies 7, 8, **A(9)**
"hat"/"line" companies 7, 8, **A(9)**
lines/ranks/files 7, 8: close order 7, 29; open order 7, 8, **A(9)**, 29, 48
volley fire 10–12
Buford, Col. Abraham 16, 40
Bunker Hill, battle of (1775) 12, 30–31, 35, 37, 44
Burgoyne, Lt.-Gen. John 18, 20, 49, 51
Butler, Lt.-Col. John 21, 22, 24

Camden, battle of (1780) 8, **A(9)**, 15, 18, 19, 37, **37**, 38, 40
cavalry/dragoon forces: (GB) 6, 7, 8, 15–16, **16**, **B(17)**, 18, **18**, 32, 35, 42, 43, 46, 60; (US) 14, 16, **16**, 21, 32, **D(33)**, 39, 41–42, **41**, 42–43, **42**, 52; (Ger) 50, 51; (Fr) 58, 60
Cedars, battle of the (1776) 24
Charleston, fall of (1781) 16, 40
Cherry Valley, battle of (1778) 22, 24
Clinton, Gen Sir Henry 7, 26
composite battalions: (GB) 8, 14; (Ger) 49
Concord and Lexington 13, 30, 37
Continental Army forces
assembling/formation 25–27, 29–30, 41
coherence/resilience of 27, 28, 30–31, 36
deployments/tactics 26, 27, 28, 29–30, 30, 31, 30–32, 34, 36, 54
drill/instruction 10, 11, 12, 26, 27, 28–29, **28**, **29**, 30, 36
fire superiority 34–35
improvements/effectiveness 36, 42, 54
Cornwallis, Lt.-Gen. Charles, Lord 8, 16, 18, 21, 37, 40, 43, 51, 52
Cowan's Ford, battle of (1781) 38
Cowpens, battle of (1781) 8, 10, 13, 15, 16, 18, 31, 32, **D(33)**, 34, 38, 40, 41, 43

d'Estaing, Comte de 56, 58
Dobbs Ferry, battle of (1778) 52

Ferguson, Maj. Patrick 14, 21, 38
Fishing Creek, battle of (1780) 16
Fort Washington, attack on (1776) 31, 50

Freeman's Farm (1777), battle of 20, 38, 51
French forces 5, 19, 48–49, 54–55, **55**, 56, **56**, 58, **H(59)**, 60, **60**

Gates, Maj. Gen. Horatio 37, 38, 40
German forces 5, 6, 24, 31, 34, 35, 44, 46–52, **G(53)**, **47**, 51
Germantown, battle of (1777) 13, 30, 36, 52
Gloucester Point, battle of (1781) 60
Green Spring, battle of (1781) 29–30
Greene, Maj. Gen. Nathaniel 27, 31–32, 34, 40, 42
Grenada, fighting on **56**, 58
grenadier battalions: (GB) 49; (Ger) 46, 47
grenadier companies: (GB) 7, 13, **13**, 14; (Ger) 47, 49; (Fr) 55
grenadier regiments: (Ger) 51
grenadiers: (Ger) **47**, 49, 52, **G(53)**; (Fr) 58, **H(59)**
Guilford Courthouse, battle of (1781) 18, 19, 31–32, **32**, 34, 37, 38, 40, 43, 48

Hamilton, Lt. Col. Alexander 44, 58
Hancock's Bridge, massacre at (1778) 40
Harlem Heights, battle of (1776) 31
Howe, Gen. William 6, **6**, 7, 8, 14, 31, 51

infantry battalions: (GB) 6, 7, 8, **A(9)**, 10–11, 29; (US) 18, 26, 27, 29–30, 34, **42**, 44; (Ger) 49, 50
infantry brigades/companies (US) 26–27, 44
infantry platoons: (GB) 8, 11; (US) 34; (Ger) 47, 49
infantry regiments: (GB) 6, 8, **A(9)**, 10, 16, **B(17)**, 24–25, 56, 60; (US) 26, 27, 34, 40, 41; (Ger) 46, 47
irregular warfare 21–22, **C(23)**, 24, 34, 38, **E(39)**, 47, 56

King's Mountain, battle of (1780) 13, 21, 38, **E(39)**
Kip's Bay, battle of (1776) 31
Knox, Col. Henry 43, **43**, 44, 61

Lee, Lt. Col. Henry 42–43
legion formations: (GB) 16, **B(17)**, 18, 21, 43, 60; (US) 41, 42–43; (Fr) 60
Lenud's Ferry, battle of (1780) 16, 38
light-infantry battalions: (GB) 13, 14, 49; (Ger) 46, 51
light-infantry companies: (GB) 6, 7, 13, **13**, 14, 16, **B(17)**, 26, 34, 52; (US) 16, 26, 36, 42, 58, **H(59)**
linear warfare 5, 6, 27, 29–30, 34, 37, 41
Long Island, battle of (1776) 14, **15**, 19, 31–32, 48, 49, 50, 52, **G(53)**
Loyalist forces 5, 8, 16, **B(17)**, 21, 22, **C(23)**, 24, 25, 35, 38, **E(39)**, 40, 42–43, 50, 56, 60

Marion, Lt. Col. Francis 38, 40, 42
Mercer, Lt. Col. John 29–30
militia forces/actions: (GB) 5, 21, 22, 35, 37, 42–43, 50, 56; (US) 5, 13, 14, 21, 22, **C(23)**, 24, 26, 30, 32, **D(33)**, 37–38, **E(39)**, 40–41, 42, 43, 47, 50, 51, 52, 56; (Fr) 56
Monck's Corner, battle of (1780) 16

Monmouth Courthouse, battle of (1777) 14, 18, 19, 26, **27**, 28, 43, 44
Morgan, Brig. Gen. Daniel 16, 32, 34, 35, 40, 43
muskets/musketry: (GB) 10–11, 12; (US) **26**, 34, 35, 36, 38, 58; (Ger) 48, **51**; (Fr) 54

Native American allies: (GB) 5, 21–22, **C(23)**, 24, 25, **25**, 35, 50; (US) 5, 24
New York campaign (1776) **5**, 14, **15**

Old Tappan, battle of (1778) 14, 40
Oriskany, battle of (1777) 24

Pandour irregulars (Ger) 46, 50
Paoli, attack at (1777) 14, 36, 40
Princeton, battle of (1777) 42, **42**, 44
Provincial forces 5, 16, **B(17)**, 21, 22, **C(23)**, 24, 25, 35, 40, 43, 60
Pulaski, Brig. Gen. Casimir 41, 42

rifle companies/regiments: (GB) 35; (US) 34
riflemen (US) 4, 34–35
rifles: (GB) 34–35; (US) 38, 51; (Ger) 51
Rochambeau, Comte de 54, **54**, 56, 60
Royal Navy actions/support 5, 6, 20, 31

Saint Lucia, fighting on 19, 56
Saratoga, battle of (1777) 13, 31, **31**, 38, 40, 51
Saratoga campaign 34, 47, 50, 63
Savannah, siege of (1779) 48, 56, 58, **60**
Schuylkill River, battle of (1777) 52
state forces (US) 5, 27, 29, 32, **D(33)**, 34, 40, 41, 43
Steuben, Friedrich Wilhelm von 12, 26, 27, **27**, 28–29, **28**, **29**, 30, 36
Stono Ferry, battle of (1779) 7
Stony Point, battle of (1779) 13, 36, 58

tactical concepts: *ordre mince* 7, 54, 56; *ordre mixte* 54, **55**; *ordre profond* 7, 54, 55
Tarleton, Lt.-Col. Banastre 16, 18, 21, 32, 42, 43, 60
Torrence's Tavern, battle of (1781) 16
Trenton, battle of (1776) 42, 44, 47, **48**, 49, 51

Valcour Island, battle of (1776) 51
Vallière system (French artillery) 61
Vigie Peninsula, battle of (1778) 19, 56

Washington, Gen. George 15, 25, **26**, 34, 41, 44
assessment of militias 38, 40
at battle of Long Island 31
at battle of Trenton 47,
cavalry protection of 42
improvement of Continental Army 26, 28
long-term strategy 63
view on rifles 35
Waxhaws, battle of (1780) 16, **B(17)**, **18**
Wayne, Brig. Gen. Anthony 29, 36
White Plains, battle of (1776) 40, 52
Wyoming, battle of (1778) **21**, 22, **C(23)**, 24

Yorktown, battle of (1781) 57, 58, **H(59)**, 60, 61, 63